"Today most of us are overindulged with material possessions. Comforts are lavished upon us by those we are close to. Yet as I talk with men and women all over the country, a frequent comment is, 'I don't feel loved or accepted.'

"In Love: No Strings Attached, *Rich Buhler presents a very clear definition of unconditional love and approval. He gives concise guidelines and the inspiration to convey true affection and approval to those around us. I know Rich personally and feel he is one of the top radio talkshow hosts in the country. He functions with knowledge of his questions and wisdom for his answers."*

Florence Littauer
Speaker
Author of Your Personality Tree

"In our fast-moving world of freeways, Rich Buhler is preaching the gospel 'where it's at'! His radio program 'Talk from the Heart' offers a tone of Christian sanity and love in the midst of jangling rock music and depressing world news.

"Now Rich's messages of love on the air waves can be gently digested in book form. Love: No Strings Attached *is filled with practical, colorful solutions on how to love ourselves, others, and the Lord.*

"The world needs Rich Buhler's valuable insights into making Christian love practical. Don't pass up this gutsy book."

Father Michael Manning
Catholic author and
television evangelist

LOVE
NO STRINGS ATTACHED

RICH BUHLER

LOVE

NO STRINGS ATTACHED

THOMAS NELSON PUBLISHERS
Nashville • Camden • Kansas City

Published in Nashville, Tennessee, by Thomas Nelson,
Inc., and distributed in Canada by Lawson Falle, Ltd.,
Cambridge, Ontario.

Printed in the United States of America.

Scripture quotations, unless otherwise indicated, are
from THE NEW KING JAMES VERSION of the Bible.
Copyright © 1979, 1980, 1982, Thomas
Nelson, Inc., Publishers.

Library of Congress Cataloging-in-Publication Data

Buhler, Rich.
  Love : no strings attached.

  1. Religious aspects—Christianity.   I. Title.
BV4639.B86   1987   241'.4   87-12178
ISBN 0-8407-7601-2

   3 4 5 6 7 8 — 92 91 90 89 88

To my parents
Henry and Genevieve Buhler

Contents

Acknowledgments

By the time a book finally gets published, there are a lot of people who have played roles in making it possible. I want to thank Paul Hanson, Dan Beach, and Al Kasha, three people who truly believed I could do it and who encouraged me in key ways; Lanny Brown for helping with transcription; Peter Gillquist for his professional input and encouragement; my editor, Janet Hoover Thoma, for taking all the pieces and actually making them into a book; my wife, Linda, and my children—Karin, Kristi, Karise, Kenny, Kevin, Kimberly, and Keith—for enduring the times I devoted to writing. I also thank the wonderful people who listen to my radio program and who have contributed so richly to my life and to this book. I am also grateful for those who attended seminars at which this material was presented and who encouraged me to put it into writing.

PART ONE

Love and Approval

Chapter One

"How Is Love Expressed in Your Home?"

One Saturday afternoon I received a call from a man who asked if I would have dinner with him that evening. "I have a lot of 'heavy' things I need to talk about," he said.

Ordinarily I would not interrupt a weekend for such a spontaneous request, but in this case I was intrigued. The caller was the son of a friend of mine. "I've been listening to your radio program for several months," he explained, "and I hope you can help me." He was referring to "Talk From the Heart," a nationally syndicated, four-hour daily talk show I host, which originates in Los Angeles.

I had never actually met Alex, the young man who had called, but I had heard stories about his life that made him take on almost legendary proportion in my mind. It was said that he had spent the last fifteen years so deeply involved in crime, drugs, and ill-gotten adventure that he had become a fugitive with international credentials.

That evening, as I waited at the table in the restaurant, I realized that this was the closest I'd ever come to meeting Pancho Villa or Al Capone. My mind became a movie camera, projecting clips of restaurant shoot-outs with Mafia machine guns, before my eyes. To make matters worse he had chosen an Italian restaurant, so I was doubly certain I was being watched by "the mob."

I needn't have worried. Alex walked in looking like a clean-cut stockbroker. Until he introduced himself I wasn't convinced he had chosen the right booth in which to sit down.

As we talked, I kept thinking, *He seems to be a very nice person . . . the kind you wouldn't mind marrying your daughter.* I tried to comprehend how he had gone from a good home to a hellish excursion in the underworld, then back to "real life" again. It didn't seem to fit.

During the course of our meal, Alex gave me an abbreviated version of his life. He had left home when he was fifteen and spent virtually every moment of his time after that living life as perversely as he could. "I worked odd jobs in construction just to get enough money to buy drugs," he said. "Eventually I started selling and became wrapped up in a racket that smuggled drugs into the United States from foreign countries." There had also been a steady stream of women in and out of his life; for a time, he said, sex had been all he lived for.

Now, at thirty years of age, he had somehow made things right with the law enforcement agencies that had come to know his past so well.

He had also become a Christian.

His conversion had been a simple and almost spontaneous one. He woke up one morning after a bout of drinking and drugs and thought to himself, *Who needs this?* He prayed for God to forgive him, confessed his trust in Christ, told his crummy friends good-bye, and a couple of days later showed up at his parents' front door.

That had been almost a year ago. Since then he had been through a drug rehabilitation program, was being discipled by his church, and was even thinking about becoming a minister. As we talked, he occasionally stopped and searched for the next word to say, a condition he said had been caused by his drug abuse. "I grieve over the fact that I no longer have the athletic, healthy body I had before all this got started."

As I listened to Alex talk, I realized that he was really returning to productive life after an absence of more than fourteen years. In some respects, he was having to begin again at thirty. His years of crime and heavy drug use had been a tragic parenthesis in his life and now, he said, he was committed to doing a lot of rebuilding.

With tears in his eyes, Alex told me that he had left home because of his father. "I don't remember a time when I felt loved by my dad. Even now the two of us are having a difficult time."

I'm not easily surprised by what people confide in me during pastoral counseling, but in this case I was stunned. Alex's father was a man of warmth and character and had on many occasions made me feel like a special person in his presence. Alex said that each of the adult children, three boys and two girls, had taken essentially the same path he had. They had left home as teen-agers, and each had become involved in drugs or alcohol. None of them was the least bit interested in a relationship with their father, and only Alex was showing any evidence of a relationship with God.

"How can I get closer to my dad?" he asked. "And how can I help my brothers and sisters understand how all this has happened?"

In the weeks that followed, Alex and I got together several times to do a bit of debriefing on what he had experienced. We covered a broad span of territory and concluded that there was not going to be any magic formula to explain all that had happened or how to solve it. But there were a couple of moments of insight, which proved to be vital and helped unlock some of the doors that seemed to stand between Alex and his father.

One of those moments came one evening when I asked Alex, "How was love expressed in your home?"

Alex thought for quite a while, then replied softly, "I don't think it was." He said it as though the thought had never before occurred to him. "I think my father has a lot of love . . . but I don't remember when or how it was ever expressed."

"When do you remember feeling anything that even resembled love, any good thing between you and your father at all?"

Alex didn't have an immediate answer to that question. As we discussed it, I gained a clearer picture of his home.

Alex's father had come from a relatively poor family but one that highly valued achievement. Sports were important, for example, as were, interestingly, fighting and self-defense. Alex's father was one of the few members of his family to get a college education, and both he and his family were intensely proud of it. Those values had been instilled in Alex's home with even greater intensity. His father loved his children, but his concern was expressed, in a contorted sort of way, by trying to get them to achieve in school, in sports, and even in fighting. Whenever any of the boys came home with a good story about a schoolyard brawl, he made them feel pretty good about whatever their role had been in it. When the boys received good grades from school and high scores in sports, they were also rewarded but not liberally.

In Alex's home there was, in my opinion, a classic example of a condition that affects many persons and many families: there was a confusion of love and approval. Let's look more closely at both love and approval and some of the ways of differentiating between them.

LOVE

Pure love is unconditional. It doesn't "depend" upon anything—whether or not I am right or wrong, short or tall, ugly or beautiful, smart or dumb, a success or failure, poor or wealthy, educated or ignorant. There aren't any strings attached to pure love, no conditions that need to be lived up to.

Pure love is given because the person "is," because the person exists. The only qualification for receiving true love is to "be."

That means that I cannot earn love. I can do nothing to improve my qualifications. I am qualified to be loved because the person who chooses to love me does so regardless of my performance and grants me love because I "am."

That, in turn, means that love cannot be lost. It doesn't depend on what I "do" to get it or what I "do" to make me lose it. Theoretically, the only way I could be disqualified as a candidate for love is to cease to "be."

One of the most powerful stories of unconditional love I've ever read is *Jungle Pilot* by Russell Hitt, which recounts the life of Nate Saint. Saint was a pilot for Mission Aviation Fellowship, an enormously effective organization that has been blazing new trails for the use of aviation in ministry to remote lands for more than forty years.

I read this book during my last year in high school, and because of my own earnest desire to seek God's will for my life and my love for aviation, the book led me to examine my own plans for the future and my own motives for life. Did I want to make a commitment to serving God? What would it mean? What choices would reflect that? The story of Nate Saint strengthened my decision to attend college and prepare for the ministry.

In the early 1950s, Nate flew small, single en- gine airplanes over vast stretches of the Amazon jungle in Ecuador. He transported missionaries to remote tribes, ferried doctors and medicines to people who would never otherwise have had them, and carried critically ill natives to city hos- pitals. In fifteen minutes he could transport a missionary over territory it had previously taken days to cover by ground or dugout canoe.

Nate's flying routine would sometimes take him over a remote, Stone-Age tribe of Indians who had come to be known as the Aucas. No out- siders had ever successfully penetrated their ter- ritory, and there were stories of how fiercely they had defended themselves from any attempts to do so. As Nate flew over their villages, however, he felt a strong sense of love for the Aucas and wanted to see the message of Christ's love brought to them.

He devised an ingenious method by which he would circle slowly over one of their villages and drop a gift to them in a bucket attached by a rope to his airplane—much-prized machete knives, chickens, anything else he thought would be of value. It didn't take long for the Aucas to show that they were looking forward to his airborne visits. A milestone came one day when Nate rolled his bucket back into the plane and discovered that the villagers had not only taken his most recent gift but placed a gift of their own into the bucket for him: a live parrot!

During the next several weeks, Nate talked with four other missionaries about the possibility of making personal contact with the Aucas. The missionaries, who were skilled linguists, would learn the obscure language of the Aucas, then put it into writing and teach the villagers how to read. Some of the missionaries would spend a lifetime translating so the Indians could have the Bible in their own language.

In preparation for this meeting, Nate experimented with landing his airplane on a sandbar in the river along one of the Auca villages. Finally, on a Wednesday in February of 1956, he flew four missionaries (Jim Elliot, Roger Youderian, Ed McCully, and Pete Fleming) and their supplies into that location. He and the missionaries soon radioed their home base to report that some young Aucas had come out of the jungle. Nate even took one of them for an airplane ride.

The following Sunday, as Nate was returning to the sandbar on a flight from the mission base, he radioed that there was a group of Aucas coming through the jungle toward the missionary camp. Perhaps this was going to be the day of their first official contact with the adult leadership of the tribe. Nate landed and joined the other four missionaries on the sandbar. They were never heard from again. A government search party later confirmed that all five had been killed in an Auca ambush, and they were later buried in the jungle a short distance from their camp.

News of the killings went around the world. Millions of people learned that these missionaries had been highly qualified, talented, and intelligent people (some of whom had been student body officers and achieving athletes) who could have succeeded in almost most anything. Their choice, however, had been to travel to a remote and anonymous part of the earth and to touch the lives of other human beings with the love that had so deeply touched their own. It was a true story of unconditional love.

But the love didn't stop there. Even though the missionary families had suffered a shattering loss, they did not pack up and return to the United States with resentment and defeat in their hearts.

Two years later two women—Rachel Saint, Nate's sister, and Elisabeth Elliot, Jim's wife, carrying her small daughter with her—walked into the Auca village and made the first successful missionary contact with the tribe. They had come with the same love fresh in their hearts and were to live with the Aucas as friends for many years to come. Rachel Saint lives in that village to this day.

Almost thirty years later, my nine-year-old son, Kenny, and I duplicated Nate Saint's last flight. We saw the airplane hangers he had built, we slept in the house he had constructed for his family, we flew his exact route to the sandbar in the river. We landed on an airstrip nearby, then walked through the jungle to Auca dugout canoes, which took us to the gravesite of the missionaries. As we stood there with a group of Auca Christians, including the son of one of the killers, we, too, felt what had brought the missionaries to Ecuador in the first place. It was a powerful experience of love.

That historic and unusual story illustrates the kind of love for which each of us hungers. It is a love that we do not have to earn and, therefore, cannot ever be lost, a love that is unconditional, given to a person because the person exists and has been chosen to be loved. No act, however criminal, can change this love.

LOVE AND APPROVAL

Approval is entirely different. Yet many people equate approval with love. Confusing the two can have a big impact on how we feel about ourselves and others.

The members of Alex's family, for example, felt the very basic need to be loved that we all feel. In their home, however, love was not visibly expressed. It was probably resident in each of their hearts, but there were not many occasions when something was said or done solely out of a motive of love. You can imagine, then, the state of personal famine that existed. Emotionally speaking the members of Alex's family were emaciated, hungering for something, anything, that would address the void they felt in their hearts.

That's when the desire for approval, in place of love, became such a powerful force in their midst.

Alex felt something warm and positive between him and his dad whenever he performed. If he brought home a good report card, he got approval and that felt good. Whenever he defended himself or someone else in a playground fight, he got approval and that felt good. It wasn't hard for Alex to come to the conclusion that in order to be loved by his father he had to perform. Alex's hunger for "being" became a matter of "doing." He came to believe that being loved depended upon what he did instead of who he was. Love and approval were not separate in his experience, so one became as though it was the other. The results were devastating.

During one of his conversations with me, Alex summarized what he had always wanted from his dad and still needed. "If my father would ever once give me the impression that he loves me just the way I am, I'd be more motivated to perform in some of the ways he expects."

Alex was longing for something from his father that was truly unconditional, that didn't depend on his having to do anything to earn it. There is a part of each of us that pleads, "Please love me just the way I am. Don't require me to become prettier or richer or smarter or thinner in order to qualify for your love."

This is the essence of genuine love. It is unconditional. The only qualification for being granted unconditional love is to "be," to exist. That's why a person's sense of being is so richly nourished by the effective expression of genuine love.

If Alex's father had come to him and looked him in the eye and said, "I love you, Son," and had done so for no other reason than the fact that he felt it and wanted to express it, Alex would have experienced pure love and an increased sense of being.

Miracles happen when ordinary human beings love unconditionally, miracles that may even continue after their deaths. A postscript to the love story of Nate Saint and his missionary friends is one example. Many years later, Kathy and Steve Saint, the teen-aged son and daughter of Nate Saint, traveled to the sandbar where their father had been slain. The two children were baptized in the river by two of the Auca men who had participated in the killing of their father and had become Christians because of his witness and the witness of his family and friends. Those two teen-agers felt the unconditional love of their dead father when Alex could not feel love from his living father. Real love will break down seemingly impossible barriers and enrich our lives way beyond our fondest dreams.

Chapter Two

"Do You Confuse Love and Approval?"

I have been in love with airplanes since my earliest years. During my junior year in college, I took flying lessons and earned my private pilot's license, but my dream was to get a commercial license, which would enable me to earn my living as a pilot. I enrolled in a respected aviation academy where my instructor, although known to be sometimes forgetful, was said to be one of the best. I worked long and hard to accumulate the necessary flying experience, pass a written examination administered by the Federal Aviation Administration, and develop the skill necessary to pass the actual flying test.

Finally, after weeks and months of accumulating more hours in the air and studying flight manuals, I was ready for the big day. The final test was given by a gruff government flight examiner and was supposed to be in two parts. The first was an oral exam; the second, an actual flight test. The examiner spread an unfamiliar chart on his desk and asked, "What do these colored lines at the top of the chart mean?" A moment of panic seized me as I fought to think. I didn't know what the lines meant.

Well, if I blow the first question, that won't cause much of a problem, I thought to myself.

Next he gave me a list of definitions to struggle with, only two or three of which I knew. He said, "You didn't study very hard for this, did you?"

Things went from bad to worse when I didn't know the answer to his third question. It was as though he was drawing from material that I had never studied. He finally settled back in his chair, sat motionless for several seconds, then reached into a desk drawer for a stack of official-looking forms. He began to write on one of them, and my heart nearly stopped as I read the words: Failure to pass.

I had dreamed about the moment he would smilingly hand me my new license, which would say Commercial Pilot. I had even arranged a celebration that evening with my instructor and a handful of friends. Now, I had failed.

Before I left that office, the flight examiner apparently found my instructor and gave him a memorable chewing-out. All I know is that as I walked out the door of the building, my instructor came to me with a sheepish look and said, "Let's get together tomorrow and talk."

We did and he admitted, "Rich, it wasn't your

fault that you couldn't answer any of the examiner's questions. The material I told you to study was for a different kind of flight test. I'm sorry."

I spent another two weeks pouring over the right materials, and the second oral exam went perfectly, as did the accompanying flight test. I finally experienced the joy of achieving my goal. The approval I had hoped for, and which had been lost, had been regained because my performance was now acceptable.

APPROVAL

As we saw in the story of Alex, the need in the human heart for approval is just about as intense as the need for love.

Approval is a smile that acknowledges a job well done.

Approval is a hug after a great achievement.

Approval is passing your commercial pilot's license test.

Every occasion of approval has one thing in common: a condition, a qualification, is required. Approval must be earned and is granted because of what a person does. Approval has to do with "doing." Approval, as I found out, can be lost.

Even though approval and love are separate and unique, some similarities can make them seem alike.

Both are hungers and, in my opinion, both are instinctive. There is something built into us that craves to be loved and craves to be approved.

Both love and approval, when they are received, have a similar result: they make us feel good. The effect is not unlike the satisfaction of a good meal when a person is physically hungry, only it is more powerful. The quenching of a hunger for love and approval not only provides a feeling of pleasure but also produces a good feeling *about me*.

An exchanging of love or a granting of approval feeds the very heart of who I am and how I feel about myself. In our desire to receive the one we will be willing to settle for the other if that is all that is available. Some of us purposely confuse love and approval.

Confusing Love and Approval

Each of us confuses love with approval in unique ways, but some experiences are common. For example, have you ever been so upset with a person that you cannot really bring yourself to express your love?

A woman asked to speak with me during a break at a weekend couples conference. She and her husband were having some strife in their marriage but nothing, I felt, that couldn't be handled with some good communication and counseling.

"How do you express love to your husband, and when was the last time you expressed your love?" I asked her. I frequently begin marital counseling with this question because the answer will often reveal if a person is confusing love and approval.

The woman seemed to miss my questions and started listing all the irritations she had stockpiled against her husband. None was imagined and each deserved to be talked about, but she was so preoccupied with them that she twice more failed to hear and answer my questions.

Finally, I stopped her in midsentence, looked her in the eye, and said, "When was the last time you told your husband you loved him?"

She was a bit startled, paused a moment, and then said, "I don't know."

During the discussion that followed, she realized that she couldn't bring herself to express any love to her husband, because there were too many things wrong in his life. She was afraid that if she really told him she loved him, he would get the impression that there was no need to change.

THE CONSEQUENCES OF
CONFUSING LOVE
AND APPROVAL

Unfortunately, many of us tend to be like this woman: we withhold love as a way of expressing disapproval. This is the first of three primary consequences of confusing love and approval. The other two are: We will interpret disapproval as a withdrawal of love, and we will grant others approval as a means of trying to give them love. All three of these consequences are harmful.

Withholding Love As a Way of Expressing Disapproval

If love and approval are essentially the same in my mind, and I treat one as the other, then it will seem logical to go on a "love strike" as a way of communicating my dissatisfaction with something in another person.

A couple of years ago I received a call from a man I'll call Henry. He was struggling with the decision of how to treat his brother, who had been a real disappointment to the family. The brother was about twenty-three, using drugs, and in and out of trouble with the law. Recently, he had decided to move in with his girlfriend, which was a shocking violation of his family's values. Most of the other family members had temporarily excommunicated him. To make matters more complex, the brother and his girlfriend had decided to get married, so the fuming relatives were having to decide whether or not to attend the wedding and, a few, whether or not actually to be members of the wedding party.

"I have decided not to be in his wedding or even go to it," Henry told me. "But I'm not sure that's right. As a Christian, what should I do?"

"How do you feel about your brother?" I asked him.

"He's the closest to me of any of the members of my family," Henry replied, "and I love him."

"Why would you refuse to be in his wedding then?"

"Because my brother has made a lot of mistakes and is not living the way he should. If I go to his wedding, I am condoning all that and saying it's okay."

I suggested to Henry that he was confusing love and approval. "It's your choice whether or not to participate in the wedding," I said, "but if you do, it would be because you love him and because you want to join in whatever happiness he feels. It does not have to mean that you approve of his choices."

"But somebody has to tell him he's doing wrong," Henry protested. "If all of us go to the wedding and act as if we love him and his girlfriend, he'll think nothing needs to change."

"Not at all," I objected. "It means one thing only—that you love him. If you don't want him to misunderstand, then you need to tell him that. You can let him know that you feel he's made some wrong choices and he's going to have to face the consequences of those choices. Tell him that you are going to be in his wedding because of your love, not because of your approval."

Henry was relieved. He wanted to do what was loving, but he had ignored this instinct because of his confusing love with approval.

If you are searching for an answer to a problem like Henry's, you might ask yourself the same questions: How do I feel about this person? What action reflects those feelings?

Sometimes your decision in a situation like this might cause you to lose all contact with the person and force that person to make a critical mistake in defiance of your lack of love. Too many parents have seen an intense and long-standing battle with their children end as the battle between Jane and her parents did.

Jane, who was raised in the religious tradition of her family, had, at the age of eighteen, befriended a boy who was a member of a dangerous cult. The parents worried about this relationship and did not approve of it. At first, they told Jane how they felt and tried to explain why. They purchased literature about the cult for Jane to read, but nothing seemed to successfully turn her attention away from the boy and what he believed.

In frustration, Jane's parents began drawing back from her. Some of their normal ways of expressing love were used less and less. Simple greetings at the dinner table or in the morning when everybody was going out of the front door came to a halt. Jane's parents made it clear that the young man was not welcome in their home, and whenever they did come into contact with him, the parents either gave him books about his cult or got into awkward disputes with him. When none of these tactics seemed to work, the parents intensified their disapproval by banning the daughter from some of the family holiday celebrations.

As you can imagine, their actions caused Jane

to identify with the feelings of persecution among the members of the cult. She was welcomed into the home of her boyfriend's parents. The girl eventually left her own faith, married the boy, and is now a committed member of his cult.

Jane's parents refused to attend the wedding, cut off all contact with their daughter, and even refused to acknowledge the birth of a grandchild.

Were the parents right to disapprove of the daughter's relationship with the boy and her interest in the cult?

Yes!

Should that disapproval have been effectively and firmly communicated to her?

Yes!

Could that have been done at the same time they expressed their love to her?

Yes!

"What if," you may ask, "Jane's parents had been faced with something even more difficult, such as Jane's announcing that she was a lesbian?" The fear that somebody important to you may be a homosexual is probably one of the biggest fears in our culture right now. Whether we approve of it or not, homosexuality is coming out of the closet. The Gay Rights Movement is campaigning for homosexuality to be accepted as an alternate lifestyle and to be protected against discrimination.

Let me say for the record that I do not approve of homosexuality. I am grieved that homosexuals are making such a concerted effort to justify and to hold on to a condition of pain and distorted sexual identity. Any attempt on the part of a person who is homosexual to get my approval will fail. I do not feel, however, that a person's homosexuality disqualifies that person from my love and from any valid help I might be able to offer, especially if that person wants help in overcoming homosexuality.

I am amazed how quickly people decide to end their friendship with someone who develops a serious problem. Although Scripture says that there may ultimately need to be a breach of friendship with a person who consciously and repeatedly chooses to do wrong, I do not believe this is to be our first response. Even when separation does occur, it is supposed to be motivated by love.

Christ loved the unlovely and prayed for the unacceptable, rather than turning away from them. The world is filled with people who decide to disassociate themselves from people with whom they disagree and of whom they disapprove. The choice of the vast majority has nothing to do with spiritual convictions or moral standards. They are merely responding to the tendency in the heart of man to pout and protest when things don't go their way. It's the adult version of the childhood expression "I'm not going to play with you anymore."

That's not even disapproval; it's intolerance. We become intolerant of those whom we disapprove and, in a self-righteous manner, we distance ourselves from them.

The Pharisees, the religious leaders of Jesus' day, advocated total separation from the people who most needed to hear their message, particularly prostitutes and tax collectors. Jesus did not condone prostitution or any other kind of promiscuity; neither did He approve of the tax collectors' apparent fraud and greed. However, He befriended these people, ate with them (which was a direct violation of pharisaicai law), showed them His love, and won their commitment to His message, a message which required them to change their ways. Jesus even said that more prostitutes and tax collectors had become His followers than religious leaders.[1]

We need to learn the skill of effectively disapproving of someone's actions without withholding our love, and I will discuss some effective ways of doing this in chapter 6.

Confusing love and approval causes pain not only for others but also for ourselves. If we confuse the two, we tend to interpret disapproval as the withdrawal of love.

Interpreting Disapproval As a Withdrawal of Love

Some people react to little criticisms as though you have just sentenced them to execution. But it's not just because the disapproval is painful; it's because they're responding to it as a withdrawal of love, which hurts even more deeply. How crazy to think that losing a game of pool or getting a C on a test or playing a wrong note at a piano recital can contribute to such an overpowering feeling of rejection, yet many of us have felt that way.

If that's how we interpret disapproval, that's how we'll react. And if we've spent our lives living on the edge of the fear of not being loved, our defenses will always respond to the slightest threat.

I'll never forget a young man who briefly associated himself with a church I pastored several years ago. I'll call him Floyd.

The first time Floyd attended my church, he seemed to be the answer to every immature pastor's dreams. During the Sunday morning message, he had his eyes riveted on me. That always makes a preacher feel good. He laughed at the right times and said "Amen" in all the right spots.

After the service he pumped my hand and told me how much he had enjoyed the service. "I've been searching for a truly fine church where I could finally feel at home," he said. "Now I've found it."

I nodded my head as Floyd talked and listened humbly to all that this unusually discerning and obviously very bright man was saying. *Oh, that more of those who sat in the pews would appreciate this church and ministry as he does,* I thought to myself.

During the next few weeks, Floyd eagerly volunteered to help, and in every way seemed like a fresh breeze in our midst. I really got caught up in his constant raving about how good our services were. Had I been an older and wiser pastor I would have seen that Floyd was a sprinter rather than a long distance runner, a vocal but shallow person.

He was also, it turned out, a good example of someone who had learned to interpret disapproval as a withdrawal of love. Floyd's credentials as the perfect church member were demolished by his actions during a series of softball games, of all things.

A few of the churches in our city got together once a week during the summer for the purpose of just having a lot of fun. We tried to give everybody a chance to play whether he was great or not.

Floyd saw things differently. He turned into an absolute churl on the softball field.

During the first game I was playing second base, and Floyd was behind me in center field. In the third inning Floyd started getting uptight, screaming at the opposing batters if he felt they were too slow. He pouted when any of our players missed the ball and would run all the way to home plate to complain to our informal umpire about what he thought were bad calls. By the end of the game, Floyd had made a real donkey of himself. We were not only disappointed but embarrassed.

After the game I pulled Floyd aside and told him that although he was welcome to participate, our league was for having fun and fellowship, not for winning the World Series, and that we all needed to keep that in mind. He was annoyed at those words and muttered, ". . . if this is an example of how the church is run, I'm not going to participate."

I missed the next game but I heard a lot about it. Floyd screamed and lectured and pouted and, at one point, had to be cooled down by the pastor of the church whose team we were playing. Similar antics popped up during the third game, and more than one of our players tried to reason with Floyd. By the middle of that game, I decided to have a stern talk with Floyd. I essentially repeated what had already been said—that we loved him, that we liked having him as a part of our fellowship, but that his conduct on the ball field had been awkward and not in the spirit of having a good time. He cursed, threw down his borrowed mitt, and left the park.

During the next weeks, several of us tried to get together with Floyd, but he did not respond to our messages. I never saw Floyd again, although I did hear from some members he had befriended that he was continuing his quest to find the right church.

The most interesting indictment from his lips was that we were "unloving" to him. He said that he had spent months looking for a church that would display genuine Christian love and had thought that he had found it. But according to him, we had treated him just as badly as the other churches.

We searched our memories and as far as we could tell, we had never had any conflict with him except on the baseball field. Yes, we did ask him to try to improve his immature behavior and made it clear that his future on the team would be affected by it.

He saw our criticism, our disapproval, to mean only one thing: we had lost our love for him (or had never loved him in the first place). For him that experience was not one of his merely failing in his performance, but an experience of his failing to "be." Our reaction was, in his eyes, not a correction of *what he did or did not do* but a rejection of *who he was.* Our disapproval was, to him, a lack of love.

It's not fun to be criticized. Disapproval always contains a measure of pain, and there probably isn't anybody who is truly immune to it (I certainly am not). Yet none of us should develop an immunity to hearing true things about ourselves. It is good for us to ask whether our reactions are really to the disapproval or to something deeper inside ourselves. At that moment are we feeling the awful loneliness of not being loved? Of not being accepted for who we are, instead of simply being corrected for what we've done?

If we confuse love with approval, it is easy for us to think of disapproval as a withdrawal of love, as a rejection of "who I am" instead of "what I did."

We've considered two of the results of confusing love and approval: (1) withholding love as a means of expressing disapproval and (2) interpreting disapproval as a lack of love. The third consequence is far reaching in its effect and can be one of the most seriously damaging: (3) granting others approval as a means of trying to give them love.

Granting Others Approval As a Means of Trying to Give Them Love

There are times, obviously, when giving approval is exactly the right thing to do. If I ask my son to wash the windows and he does the job satisfactorily, I will give him my approval. If he does not wash the windows to my satisfaction, however, it is important that I express my disapproval and tell him how to correct the problem so he can do a better job next time. Some of us feel guilty about expressing any kind of disapproval, no matter how much it is deserved, because we fear that expressing disapproval is an unloving act. Sometimes we even go so far as to grant our approval to people who haven't earned it, because we convince ourselves that giving such unearned approval is actually an act of love.

One afternoon on my radio program I received a call from a frustrated mother of three. The reason for her call, she said, was to get some advice about her children. She described two boys and a girl who were essentially out of control and wouldn't do much of anything that was required or asked of them. The mother's specific question was, "How can I get them to do their chores and to help around the house?"

I started formulating some answers in my mind and making other inquiries to help clarify details about her and her family. The more I asked, however, the more suspicious I got about her "children."

I finally queried, "How old are your children?"

I could imagine I heard gasps throughout the listening audience as she said, "My two sons are twenty-two and twenty-eight, and my daughter is twenty-five."

It was a horror story. All three were on drugs. The two boys had been in trouble with the law. None of them had steady work, and there was a stack of telephone bills, credit card slips, and gasoline receipts that would have made J. Paul Getty gulp. That did not include actual cash the parents had handed out to the three as either loans or gifts.

"We just can't do it anymore," the mother said.

It didn't take King Solomon or a Ph.D. in psychology to know what this dear mother and her husband should do.

"You're going to have to stop financially subsidizing the irresponsibility of these three adults. Let them carry the load of life themselves," I advised her. "They need to be cut loose."

For starters I suggested she suspend the credit card privileges immediately, tell them to install their own telephones with their own money, and let them know that if they wanted money for cars, gas, parties, they would have to get very creative as to where they were going to get it—finding a job might be a step in the right direction. I also recommended she tell them that although she loved them and would go through almost anything *with* them, she was no longer going to go through things *for* them. In other words, if they got into trouble, they would have to be prepared basically to bear the consequences themselves.

That mother and I spent more than twenty minutes discussing the situation. My point was very clear: Let them grow up. Let them live in the real world, a world where Mom and Dad are not going to let destructive things interfere with the sense of responsibility the three kids would have to develop.

When my discourse was finished, there was a tense silence. Then, in a quiet voice, she said, "But that wouldn't be loving."

In this mother's mind, love was conveyed by making her children feel good, and she had always done that by giving them whatever they wanted and by avoiding any criticism of them. She had considered it unloving to say "No" to their requests for money or to turn down paying for their car insurance or bailing them out of jail. Now she was faced with the painful consideration of actually kicking them out of her house, but that seemed like such an unloving thing to do that she couldn't conceive of ever doing it.

Both this woman and her husband loved their children deeply. They had wanted them, prayed over them, and sacrificed a lifetime for them. They had not distinctly expressed their love, however, by hugging or kissing or just saying "I love you." The way they had communicated their love was through carte blanche approval.

Isn't it interesting how we can flip-flop love and approval and make them just the opposite of what they are? We know that love means doing something unconditional, so we offer unconditional approval! The results of that, however, can be devastating both to the person giving the approval and to the person receiving such approval.

Love does not mean never having to say you're sorry, as the old movie so romantically proposes. Instead, my son can say, "I'm sorry that I did a sloppy job of washing those windows, Dad," and still know that he's loved by me today and tomorrow, as long as we both live. My unconditional love gives him that security.

PART TWO

Love

Chapter Three

"How Do I Express Love?"

In fifteen years of pastoral counseling, I have sat across the desk from or shared a cup of coffee with a lot of people who are going through tough times. Sometimes it is a husband and a wife who are finally venting years of resentment. Often they are separated or getting a divorce. Other times it is a kind of in-house warfare between parents and children.

I think I've probably dealt with almost every category of conflict that can exist between people, and early in my experience I noticed something fascinating: even when people are fighting and scrapping and threatening to disown each other, love is lurking down inside of them.

I'll never forget two people whom I will call Jack and Mary. Late one night, a mutual friend of theirs had called me and asked if I would consider talking with them. This was the second marriage for both Jack and Mary, and they had been married to each other for sixteen years.

They arrived at my office showing signs of their long battle. Jack was the rough-and-tough and hard-to-bluff type. He kept his jaw clenched and had a tendency to look at the floor as he talked. Mary seemed numb. She looked as if she had completely fallen to pieces but had been hastily thrown together for our meeting.

The more we talked the more I realized that these two people genuinely loved each other. Like most of us, each had the desire to be loved and to be loving, to have a happy home, to be married to a happy mate.

I looked at Jack and said, "If you came home one evening and found the house on fire and you knew that Mary was inside, would you risk your life trying to get her out?"

Admittedly, it was a terribly emotional question, which measured more Jack's attitude about life and death than his feelings about his wife, but the inquiry produced some interesting results. Jack fidgeted in his chair, looked at me, looked at the floor, glanced at Mary, and then started trembling. He wrestled to hold his emotions, but his moist eyes and the tears that began running down his cheeks gave an indication of his answer.

I turned to Mary. "Mary, if you came home and found the house on fire, would you risk your life trying to get Jack to safety?"

With a gesture of mock disgust, Mary reached

over and grasped Jack's hand. They both sat there, not quite knowing what else to say. They'd die for one another. (They just couldn't *live* with one another!) They both knew it. They had founded their marriage in love; both of them had committed themselves to love; and even in this disintegrating stage of their marriage, each loved the other. But the more I talked with them the more obvious it was that the love they felt for one another had never been truly and distinctively expressed. Their problem was not a lack of love. It was, in part, a lack of expression of love.

We've talked about the importance of distinguishing between love and approval and of expressing these two different aspects of a relationship in ways that, at times, reflect that distinction.

The question, "What are the best ways to express love and approval?" now needs to be answered. How can I be sure that the love I want to give is going to be received as love and not as approval? And vice versa?

EXPRESSION OF LOVE

If we asked a thousand people what best expresses love to them, we would end up with several areas of agreement.

For example, most of us would probably emphasize the importance of expressing love verbally, saying "I love you."

Others might mention the need for expressing

love through touch, physical contact. The first time I ever met the famous speaker and author Charlie "Tremendous" Jones, he gave me a big bear hug and said, "We all need at least seven of those a day to thrive."

That's how I used to summarize the expression of love: verbal and physical. In pastoral counseling, I would talk about how hungry each of us is to hear someone say "I love you" and how basic it is to give someone a hug or a kiss or another physical expression of love.

But I've come to realize that the expression of love needs to go much beyond that.

What is love, exactly?

Is it a feeling?

Is it a virus that afflicts people at random and either you've got it or you haven't?

Through the centuries people far better than I have tried to define love, so I don't know why I should accept the challenge, too. But for the sake of our treatment of the subject I'm going to do it.

Here is the Rich Buhler definition of love: *Love is anything done for a person because of who that person is.*

Yes, there are emotions of love, wonderful feelings that accompany our decision to love someone. But unless all those surges of alleged commitment rise up and out of us into words or deeds, they don't really mean very much.

One of my most memorable calls on the radio came from a soft-spoken young woman who was concerned about her relationship with her boyfriend. Like many dating single people, she was trying to figure out where it all was headed. Were they growing together? Were they drifting apart? Was this friendship ever going to lead to marriage?

I asked her if she loved her boyfriend.

Yes, she did.

I asked her if her boyfriend loved her.

She said she thought so.

I asked her how her boyfriend expressed his love to her.

She was stuck for an answer.

"Has he ever said that he loves you?"

"No," she said.

"Have you ever asked him if he loves you?"

"I've tried but he doesn't seem to be able to answer that question."

"Have you ever complained to him about his lack of expressing love?"

She said that she had but that he had gotten angry and told her, "You ought to be able to figure that out for yourself."

Are you ready for the clincher?

They had been "going together" steadily for more than seven years!

I don't know about you but I think a man who spends seven years in this kind of a relationship with someone and never expresses his love to his alleged girlfriend isn't worth having. I don't know what feeling he did have for her, but it wasn't love.

Of course, the girl had problems of her own for holding on to a situation like that. But the point is that if we had hauled that boyfriend into court and charged him with loving her, there wouldn't have been enough evidence to convict him! He'd never done anything to show his love for her.

Love is not an intention that dwells sincerely, but safely, somewhere in our hearts.

Love is something that we actually do for the person whom we love, for the purpose of simply responding to who that person is.

As you can see, this definition focuses on the *motive* for an act of love rather than the *kind* of act that is performed. That definition evolved out of a counseling experience at a summer camp for college students.

Hugs and Kisses Do Not Always Express Love

One of the young singles attending the camp was a girl named Becky, a delicate blond with neatly trimmed short hair and sharp features. She was the type of person whose clothes always looked as if they had never been worn before.

Becky asked if she could chat with me about a concern in her life, so I arranged to meet her at a picnic table under the pine trees.

I won't go into all the details except to say that the more she talked, the more convinced I became that she was a classic product of a home that had confused love and approval.

Then I asked the question, "How was love expressed in your home?"

I didn't hear what I expected. She said that there had been a lot of hugs and kisses and verbal expressions of love in her home—all the ingredients that I was convinced couldn't have been there.

"Oh, no," I heard myself say. "That's not possible."

I had been thinking, *You see, I've got it all figured out. Love and approval are different and, uh, you are obviously suffering from a confusion of them. . . !*

I was stuck. I had found a person who did not fit into my clever way of viewing things!

For more than a half hour Becky documented what she had already said: she could remember the warmth of hugs and kisses and her parents saying "I love you." Yet the meaning of those gestures and the kind of effect one would expect were not in her life.

And there was a good reason. Yes, she could remember a hug or a kiss here and there, and she recalled being told "I love you." But those things only occurred on occasions of approval.

She searched her memory but could not recall a single instance when love was expressed apart from a good report card or a home run or a "10" in gymnastics or a cleaned room or a mopped kitchen floor.

Did love exist in her home? The answer is "Yes." Were the things she experienced uplifting and approving? Once again the answer is "Yes." Were they distinct expressions that she was valued for "who she is"?

That answer is definitely "No."

Becky's story illustrates an important principle: No particular act automatically expresses love. We generally associate kisses and hugs and certain phrases with the expression of love, but they don't always mean that. Whether or not an action is a genuine expression of love depends on the motive for the act.

For example, if I give you a nicely wrapped package with an expensive watch inside, what does that mean? Does it mean I love you? Does it mean "Congratulations, you did a great job"?

The truth is that you don't know exactly what it means. It depends on what my motive is for giving it. If I give you the watch for no other reason than just to say "I love you," then you will see it as an expression of love. If I give it as a reward for something you have done, then you will see it as an expression of approval. It could have meant other things, such as, "Forgive me" or "I'd like to get to know you" or "Good-bye."

The first measurement of whether something is an act of love or of approval is, What is the motive for that act? This focuses on *why* I've done something rather than on *what* I've done.

If you sit and think about that for a bit, the effect can be quite sobering. It was for me. I was convicted in my own heart for the times I had pretended to be offering love to people around me when my conduct really meant something else.

Becky realized that she could probably write a dictionary of what the phrase "I love you" really meant at various times in her family. Instead of its meaning "I value you for who you are," it sometimes meant "You did a great job cleaning your room" or "Thanks for bringing home such a good report card" or "That meal tasted wonderful." In other words, it usually meant "I approve of your performance," and Becky learned that if she ever wanted some of those seeming expressions of love, she had to do certain things to earn them.

Sometimes when we think we're lavishing love on others, we're not acting very loving at all. We're not saying, "I love you because of who you are" but rather, "I'm really hurting inside and have to smother you with all these things that I think are love but which are really something other than love." How often, for example, has the phrase "I love you" been used when what was actually meant was "I want something from you" or "I want to hear you say that you love me so I can say I love you, even though I really don't feel that way"?

Loving Gifts

Once we realize that unconditional love is expressed by the giver's motives, we are free to show love in some ways that have sometimes been criticized as being poor expressions of love. How many times have you heard someone say, for example, "Joe gives his kids all kinds of gifts because he's trying to make up for something"? The implication is that the giving of gifts, especially if they are expensive, somehow falls short of being a valid expression of love. The truth is that gifts can be valid expressions of love, depending on the motive for which they were given.

A flower can say "I love you."

A gift certificate can say "I love you."

A trip to Europe can say "I love you."

A pack of gum can say "I love you."

Virtually anything can say "I love you" if the reason for its being given is actually one of love.

The challenge to our hearts, then, is first to define love, which I suggest is anything I do for another person because of who that person is. No other hidden agenda or motive. I just want to validate the person. Then I am on better footing for actually getting about the business of expressing love verbally.

THE LANGUAGE OF LOVE

Is it sufficient to have a right motive? If my heart is sincere, am I expressing love adequately? Many of us think so, especially if we are the person giving the love. As long as we are satisfied that our hearts are right, we tend to feel that we've done our job. If the other person can't feel or doesn't receive our love, that's not our problem.

Unfortunately, our most sincere attempts to express love often don't succeed. One of the reasons can be found in looking at what I call "the language of love."

The language of love consists of all the ways that a person has discovered for expressing love. We learn that language from our homes, from our friends, from watching other people, from television, from films, from newspapers, books, and magazines. Anytime we have either experienced what we think is love or have seen it in the lives of others or have heard stories about it, we have added to our language of love.

Each of us has his or her own uniquely developed language of love. If you and the person you married were born on the same day in the same hospital, lived next door to one another in the same city, attended the same schools and church, and graduated from the same college, you would still be like two people from foreign countries who speak different languages. Even children who grow up in the same family come away with their own, unique languages of giving and receiving love.

Unfortunately few of us realize this language barrier. Since we've spent a lifetime developing a language of love, we tend to think that everyone in the world speaks the same language—ours. Everyone, that is, except the person we married!

I once counseled a couple I'll call Dan and Sue, who spent a weekend together at a marriage retreat where I was the guest speaker. The first night I arrived, one of the leaders of the group said he hoped there would be an opportunity for me to talk with them, because he felt they were having some real problems.

The next morning Dan and Sue approached me and asked to get together during the afternoon break. They had been married fifteen years, had three children, and were committed

Christians, but they were going through a tough time in their marriage.

As we talked it was apparent to me that they loved one another and wanted to make a go of their marriage. They had accumulated a lot of resentment, however, and were considering a separation.

I asked Sue that important question, "How do you express your love to Dan? What little things do you do to say you care?"

She glanced at the other end of the long couch where Dan was sitting, then turned to me and said, "I like flowers and I think they are romantic. From time to time I'll go out in the garden, cut a rose, put it into a special vase, and put it on his nightstand." Then she added, "Sometimes that's my way of telling him that I'd like to make love."

"Sue, you're a romantic!" I told her. "That's a wonderful and tender thing to do."

Then I turned to Dan. "What does that mean to you, Dan?"

"Nothing," he replied.

I thought Sue was going to jump across the couch and claw his eyes out!

"What did you think whenever you saw a flower pop up on your nightstand?" I asked.

"I just thought it meant Sue liked flowers. I didn't know."

Dan was looking a bit sheepish by now. Yet he was not the only one who misunderstood his partner's language of love.

"How do you express your love to Sue?" I

asked Dan. "What do you do to say that you care?"

Before Dan could answer, Sue looked at him with an "I-know-what-you're-going-to-say-and-I'm-not-going-to-like-it" look.

Dan quietly shared a story that I did not expect to hear. Sue was a professional person and worked hard; sometimes he felt bad about all the pressures that were upon her as a working wife and mother. Whenever Sue was away for the evening or had gone to bed early, Dan would scour the house, pick up all the dirty laundry, put it through the washing machine, transfer it to the dryer, and eventually fold it and put each piece of clothing in its rightful place.

It was one of the most practical ways of expressing love and care I had ever heard. "Dan, if we filled an arena with twenty thousand women, they would mob you in admiration for being the kind of man who did not come up with something corny as a way of expressing love."

Sue, however, was so flushed with anger that I could have cooked an egg on her forehead. Her frustration obviously revealed one key to their problems.

"Tell me how you feel about that," I asked her.

Sue began by telling me how capably she had fulfilled her responsibilities as a wife and mother until a few years ago when she had suffered a serious back injury and had to have surgery. She had spent almost a year in traction, completely immobilized. The doctors feared at times that she would never walk again.

The whole experience had been an emotional and painful one, she said, "But one of the hardest parts was lying in bed and being cared for by others. Day after day, month after month, I had to watch other people, family members and volunteers, take care of my children. At my worst moments I felt that I would never be needed in my home again. My family had learned to live without me."

For the past several months Sue had shown encouraging signs of recovery. Although she was not yet working, she was able to get out of bed and do a few things around the house. Two of the chores she enjoyed most were doing the dishes and, you guessed it, washing the clothes. Just doing these two things proved to her that she was recovering physically and made her feel useful as a wife and mother. She appreciated what Dan was trying to do for her, but at this stage in her life it was almost an act of thievery. "I've tried to explain this to Dan," Sue said, "but he never seems to hear what I'm saying." Here was a classic example of how one person's act of love can end up putting another person in a prison.

Love cannot be truly expressed unless we first understand the other person's language of love. I hate to pick on the husbands, but I've got to tell another classic story of the breakdown in the language of love.

Several years ago I was a staff member at a large church. Shirley, one of the older women, came to me two or three times to talk about some pressures in her marriage and in her relationship with her grown children. One afternoon she said casually that in more than thirty years of marriage her husband, David, had not bought her a birthday present, a Christmas present, or an anniversary present.

I couldn't believe it.

I interrupted what she was about to say next and asked, "How does that make you feel?"

Her eyes filled with tears, and for the next several minutes, she let decades of pain and resentment flow out.

I couldn't help thinking to myself, *What a jerk her husband must be never to give any gifts on special occasions.* He was not a Christian or a churchgoer so I'd never met him, but from afar I decided not to like him!

About a year later I got a call from the husband who asked if he could make an appointment to talk with me. He said that he knew his wife had been talking with me and that he would like to do the same.

A part of our time together was spent talking about his relationship with his wife. It was natural for me to ask him my usual question and at the same time satisfy my curiosity about his unusual attitude toward gift-giving. "How do you show your love for your wife? Do you give her gifts?"

Guess what? He had a good explanation.

The man had been reared in a family where there was a lot of abuse. "Everybody spent most of their time either fighting with or enduring one another," he said. "Then when Christmas or birthdays came around we had to go through the ritual of buying gifts which, to me, seemed meaningless. I vowed that I would never give gifts just because they were expected. I wanted to give a gift when it would really mean that I cared." He had given hundreds of gifts to his wife through the years, but none of them had corresponded with Christmas or birthdays or anniversaries.

I had to admire a person who came into his marriage committed to experiencing something more real than his own childhood. Nevertheless he was wrong not to consider his wife's language of love. She had some measure of appreciation for his sincere giving, but according to her language, she was still starving for love. If this man had really wanted her to feel his love, he needed to know her language of love and use it to express his love.

There's a footnote to this story, by the way. Not only did David fall completely short of Shirley's language of love in terms of the occasions for gift-giving, but he also blew it when it came to the kinds of gifts he gave.

Shirley wanted to receive pretty cards and decorative ceramics. David didn't see much value in those "trinkets," however. He wanted to express his caring in ways that really "counted." Because he had suffered poverty as a child, this successful businessman felt that the most important thing he could provide for his wife was financial security. *Surely*, he thought, *she would appreciate that more than trinkets*. So whenever he felt like telling her of his love, he would bring home certificates of gold futures or stock options. His wife may have sat out a lot of Christmases, but she was hot stuff on the stock market!

Once again there was an element of logic and love in what he had done, but his motive wasn't matching his wife's expectations. That left her frustrated. Whenever she tried to explain how she felt, he thought she was accusing him of not loving her so he would defend his actions. Their discussions turned into arguments before they ever understood what the other was saying.

During the first years of our own marriage my wife, Linda, would occasionally tell me how much it meant to her for me to continue to observe some of the etiquette of courting. For instance, if we were getting into the car, she wanted me to take the trouble to go over to her side of the car and open the door for her. If you had asked me if I knew that was important to her, I would have answered, "Yes." If you had asked me how high on her list of ways of expressing love it was, I would have said, "Oh, about number 32."

That's because it was about that low on my own list. If you would have told me that opening the car door for her was *third* on my wife's list of priorities, I would have told you to get lost. After all, I knew my wife better than you. But it was third on her list!

I was blown away when I first learned that. It meant that if I wanted to express my love and care in a way that was important to her, a simple act like opening the car door would do it.

The sad truth is that at that time I seldom expressed my love in this way. What would I do? I'd call her from work saying, "Get a babysitter. I'm taking you out for dinner tonight."

Every girl likes to be taken out to dinner, right? Every girl likes to do something spontaneous and goofy, right? Oh, how lucky I considered her to be that her husband would brighten her evening by substituting a cozy little table for two for the family dinner table. How I grieved for all the unlucky women who did not have a sensitive and fun-loving husband like me.

And how Linda loathed it all!

After several years of this, Linda finally broke the news that although she occasionally enjoyed going out for a nice meal, and there were times when she considered that romantic, she basically didn't like dropping everything on the spur of the moment and leaving the kids in disarray.

I think all these stories are fairly self-explanatory. Each of us has a language of love that is unique, distinct. We use it to express love to others, and we expect others to use it to express love to us. When that doesn't happen we fear that love may have been lost.

But what if we feel that we are illiterate when it comes to speaking the language of love? Is there hope?

Chapter Four

"How Do I Learn the Language of Love?"

It is a victorious day in our lives when we come to realize that our language of love is not the only one in the universe and that the person we love may be tuned into a completely different frequency. However, that insight is just the beginning. Once I've acknowledged that my language of love and another person's language are different, what do I do about it? How can I learn another person's language of love, and how can I teach mine to another person?

The simple answer is "Ask!"

The only way we're going to find out what hidden expectations lurk in the hearts of those we love is to sit down and talk about them. It's fascinating, though, how many obstacles can stand in the way of such a conversation. One of these I've already mentioned in the previous chapter.

Because each of us has spent a lifetime developing a language of love from many sources, we miss the fact that ours is a relatively unknown language. That's why it's so easy to have the mistaken feeling that there is an accepted, authorized, universal language of love that every "normal" person speaks and understands.

It's a lonely feeling, then, if after several months or years of marriage, we reluctantly come to the conclusion that our spouse somehow missed out on the language lessons. We married a functional illiterate when it comes to expressing love. We don't want to talk about the "little" expectations we've had and the hurt that has resulted from the things our mate doesn't do to reinforce our love because, in our mind, they shouldn't have to be talked about.

It's easy to have the feeling that "If he were really a wise, sensitive husband, then he would just *know*. Nobody should have to tell him." Or, "If she were really 'tuned in' to men, then she'd respond the way I want."

We act as though talking about these things will somehow pop the bubble. The magic will be gone. We can make the choice not to open up our hearts if we want to, but we'll also be making the choice to continue living in the isolation of our disappointment and the resentment that accompanies it. What that amounts to is a shifting of responsibility. Instead of fuming over the fact that what we had hoped would happen didn't happen and holding the person who failed to meet our expectations responsible, we need to accept responsibility for our own unhappiness. We must realize that we are the only ones who can change the situation by communicating to the other person how we're feeling and what specifically can be done about it.

An experience in my own growing-up years is a simple example of what I'm talking about. One year my birthday happened to fall during the week that a bunch of us kids were at summer camp. I didn't think much about it until we sang "Happy Birthday" to one of the campers one morning at breakfast. Suddenly it struck me that in just two days it would be my own birthday, and I was fairly sure that nobody in the whole camp knew it. The more I thought about it the sadder I got.

The morning of my birthday I got up without fanfare and went through the routine of getting ready for breakfast. But on the inside I was having an absolute pity party. Here I was in the midst of total strangers, far away from home on my special day, and everyone here thought this day was the same as any other.

As I took my shower I hoped that people might really know it was my birthday. They weren't saying anything, I thought, because they were going to surprise me at breakfast.

No such luck. Breakfast that morning was the same as usual.

Maybe, I thought, *there will be a miracle. Maybe one of the counselors will have a vision saying, "Today is Rich Buhler's birthday. Be kind to him." Or maybe somebody in the office will suddenly and without explanation have the urge to go through the registration forms and notice my birth date. He or she will say to the other staff members, "Here's a poor little camper who is having a birthday today. Let's do something special for him." Or perhaps my parents are going to surprise me at dinner with a cake and some gifts they've sent from home!*

I didn't want to tell anybody. That wouldn't be right. If I told somebody it was my birthday, then they might feel obligated to say or do something. I would be arranging my own party.

By midafternoon when we were playing baseball, I couldn't stand it anymore. I let it slip to one of my teammates that it was my birthday. Within thirty seconds the whole playing field was filled with the familiar strains of "Happy Birthday." That night the campers sang to me at supper. I had learned an important lesson. I couldn't expect people around me to be mind readers, and I couldn't hold the world accountable for not knowing what I felt or what would help me feel better.

Each of us needs to realize that we must communicate our expectations effectively to those who are in the best position to respond to them.

For married couples, I recommend a valuable project, which will help each person first to discover his or her own language of love and then to share it with the other.

IDENTIFYING THE LANGUAGE OF LOVE

Initially, each person spends some time alone, putting together two separate lists. The first: The Ways I Expect to Receive Love. The second: The Ways I Communicate Love.

When you are making lists remember that little things mean a lot. Some of the greatest delight comes from soft, quiet, and almost invisible expressions of love. And some of the deepest pain results from the lack of these same little things. I've seen many couples' lists, and some of the priority items include things like a simple glance across the room or a surprise phone call at work or a hug in the middle of the night or being thoughtful enough to use deodorant before coming to bed. You may need to spend several days occasionally going back to your lists and adding anything else that comes to mind.

Once your lists are complete, go through each list and as best as possible rank each item in order of importance. What is most important to you? Second most important?

Most husbands and wives are usually aware of something that the other considers to be an expression of love. But I find that couples are constantly stunned to find out, by comparing and ranking, how important some of those things are to one another.

After you and your mate have done this, sit

down and compare your lists, taking note of the top five or ten items on your husband's or wife's list. The next time your heart is in the mood to say "I love you," consider one of those ways.

A RADIO SURVEY

I once asked the persons in my radio audience to send me some examples of their own languages of love. I received more than fifteen hundred responses from both men and women, and the results were interesting.

The women appreciated things like:

My husband's bragging about me to friends.
His remembering a special day.
His calling from work to say "I love you."
His washing the dishes for me.
His taking me for a special night out.
His preparing a special meal so I don't have to.
His looking at me across the room at a party.
His sending me a "Peanuts" card.
His complimenting me on my appearance.
His realizing when I need space.

The men appreciated:

My wife's giving me a surprise in my lunch.
Her taking interest in my hobbies.
Her accepting my advice.
Her initiating sex.
Her defending my reputation.
Her rubbing my feet.

The Most Frequent Responses

There were hundreds of unique expressions, some of which occurred only once in fifteen hundred responses. For the sake of simplicity we went through the lists and arranged the responses in broad categories, such as verbal expression of love, physical expression of love (hugs and kisses), gifts, being listened to, sex, unconditional acceptance.

We were interested in seeing how often certain items occurred no matter how high or low they were on a person's list. Women mentioned hugs and kisses more than any other category; being listened to the next most often. (I've taken surveys during dozens of marriage conferences, and this has consistently been an important hunger among wives.) The third most often listed category was verbal expression of love.

The most frequently mentioned category for the men was the same as for the women: the expression of love through hugs and kisses. The second most often mentioned item for men was unconditional acceptance. (That, too, is consistent with what I have seen in similar surveys among married couples. The women have the hunger to be heard, to be taken seriously, and the men have the hunger to be accepted just as they are.)

The Top Priorities

Next, we went through the fifteen hundred responses and determined how important, on the average, various categories were. How high in men's and women's priorities did particular items rank?

Among women, the overall highest ranking category was unconditional acceptance. Among men, the highest ranking was verbal expression of love. Sex, interestingly, ranked exactly the same on both men's and women's lists—the fifth most important category out of the ten that we asked them to rate.

This survey is far from scientific, but it is interesting. I present it in order to give some examples of the languages of love and categories that are important. What you or your mate considers important may not resemble anything on this list. It is a mistake to say, "This is the way 'women' are" or, "This is the way 'men' are." You need to determine, "This is the way my wife is" or, "This is the way my husband is." Don't assume that you know!

I am often asked, "What if my mate won't participate in this kind of project?"

My answer is, "Don't let that stop you from making lists of your own language of love." You will benefit from putting serious thought into the ways that you express love or should express love. You may decide to go ahead and share your lists with your mate anyway. Also, it will be valuable to realize that your mate does have a language of love, even if you have to speculate what it is.

"I always viewed my husband as an unexpressive and unaffectionate person," one woman once told me. "Your discussion about the language of love made me realize that he does a lot of things which are probably his own way of saying that he cares, but I've never viewed them as that."

The Language of Christmas

Each of us has other languages in our lives that are just as important for us to learn and to know about one another.

For example, each of us has our own language of Christmas. For me, Christmas is not Christmas without a fluffy white Christmas tree with color-coordinated decorations. However, for my wife, Christmas is a freshly cut green tree with traditional decorations. When we first married, we had to come to grips with the fact that each of us had spent our lives developing completely different Christmas customs. In her home Christmas gifts were simple, practical, and inexpensive. In my home the gifts were never lavish but they were of a different variety from that to which she was accustomed. In her home the "stockings were all hung by the chimney with care," and on Christmas morning there were gifts from Santa Claus. In my home we didn't hang Christmas stockings, and we didn't pretend that Santa was real. So Linda and I had some adjusting to do.

The Language of Sex

Each of us also has a unique language of sex. Both men and women commonly come into their marriage expecting the sexual relationship to be everything they've always dreamed and their mate to fit right into their fantasies. When that doesn't happen, many spouses feel isolated, as though they were cursed with a partner who just didn't attend the same school when it came to sex. Couples need to talk openly about their physical relationship, to know one another's language of sex, and to review together some of what has contributed to each language.

I recall counseling with a young man I'll call Ralph. He was in his late twenties and had been married for about six years. His wife had urged him to talk with me. "She feels that things could be better in our sexual relationship," Ralph said, "and we've had so much conflict over the subject that I finally agreed to talk with someone about it."

I had compiled a questionnaire on the language of sex, which I used for a couples conference. I gave copies to Ralph and asked him and his wife to fill it out and then to discuss it together.

"We've discovered some amazing things," Ralph told me later. "I guess I was influenced by things I heard my mother say when I was growing up. I actually had the impression that women just don't enjoy sex very much. I was so convinced of that, I would never really allow a free relationship with my wife. I was always afraid of doing something to turn her off, so I went the other direction and did very little at all."

Ralph said their sex life had been character-ized by very brief sexual encounters, which left his wife feeling frustrated and wondering why her husband didn't want to invest more time in their physical relationship. "She started feeling like she wasn't attractive to me," Ralph said. In addition, Ralph remembered some childhood sexual experiences that had left him feeling con-fused and dirty and would require some good counseling to overcome. Our discussions helped Ralph realize that his reluctance toward sex with his wife was not only because of how he thought she felt, but also because of some hindrances in his own heart. Over a period of time both Ralph and his wife were able to explore the hunger each of them had to share sexually and to make one another aware of their languages of sex.

The Language of Lifestyle

There are also languages of lifestyle. For exam-ple, I have never been too particular about the kind of house I live in. I'd make a great mission-ary!

Linda, on the other hand, has a language of lifestyle in which the kind of house we live in makes a big difference. The kitchen window has to be in just the right place, the house has to be facing the right direction, the number of walls has to be in the right proportion to the number of windows, and so on.

Early in our marriage when we would look at a house to rent, I would be willing to take almost anything, but she would be more fussy and that used to frustrate me. I even arrogantly considered it to be a spiritual problem on her part. I'd think to myself, *If only she were flexible and able to accept whatever the Lord gives us*. The truth is, however, that she and I have two different languages when it comes to renting or buying a house. Frankly, hers is a lot more practical than mine. When I finally realized that this difference between us was not the result of a deficiency on her part, it saved a lot of heartache.

In my lifestyle gadgets are important. If it beeps and runs on batteries, I'll probably like it. I'm into computers, electronics, and airplanes. Linda doesn't understand my interest in gadgets and has sometimes even resented it.

She, on the other hand, loves to shop in fabric stores. I don't know how anyone can go into a store where there are four hundred bolts of cloth and choose which one to buy, but Linda loves it. She knows the location of every fabric store within forty miles of our house.

When we both realized how important fabrics and gadgets were to each other, we tried to understand one another's interests. In fact, I now like fabric stores because she loves them so much. And she has actually bought me a few gadgets as gifts!

It is vital that each of us steps outside our own

view of things and realizes that the people we love sometimes see things differently. It *is* an act of love to take the time to learn another person's language and to use that knowledge to develop a better relationship. Instead of a couple's spending their lives together speaking Swiss and German to each other, they will develop their own new language, just as the Swiss developed a special form of German, Swiss German, which has been their unique language for centuries.

PART THREE

Disapproval

Chapter Five

"Isn't It Wrong to Express Disapproval?"

If all we ever had to do in life was to make people feel terrific by loving and approving of them, we'd have it made. There is another side to relationships, however, which is as important as love and approval but which isn't as much fun to express. That's disapproval.

Most of us don't like to communicate disapproval to others. And we certainly don't like others to tell us that they disapprove of what we are doing. Some of us avoid criticism at all costs.

There are a lot of reasons for that. One is the fear that disapproval may mean there is something wrong with the relationship. Many of us enter into marriage, for example, with the romantic ideal that a perfect couple will virtually never disagree and will rarely express disapproval of one another. If disapproval is communicated, some of us panic: Maybe the relationship is on the verge of breaking up!

Another reaction to disapproval is one we have already talked about: the fear that disapproval means a lack of love. If every time you criticize me I think you are saying that you don't love me, then my defenses will be at their peak.

FEAR OF HURTING ANOTHER PERSON

The biggest reason we avoid disapproval, however, is because it involves pain. Saying something honest and confrontive to another person about that person's fault or failure will hurt, and somehow it doesn't seem right to hurt someone we love. Some of us actually make that a principle of life: Love means never inflicting pain. For others it's a matter of spiritual commitment: Christians are always loving, even to their enemies, so for me to say something critical to someone is not Christian.

Whatever the reason, any decision on our part to avoid accepting or communicating disapproval is going to have a harmful impact on relationships, since the effective expression of disapproval is a vital part of loving one another.

Not long ago I received a call on the radio from a woman who said, "I love my husband and he's a good man in many respects, but when he comes home from a hard day of work as a carpenter, he doesn't shower." She said he would just plop himself in front of the television, eat the evening meal, and then putter in the garage until late, when he would bring his smelly body to bed.

I asked her, "What does he say when you talk with him about this?" There was a long silence during which I could imagine thousands of radio listeners turning up their volume to hear her answer.

"I've never really mentioned it to him," she said.

I could then imagine those listeners asking, "Why not?" I couldn't believe it myself.

The more we talked the clearer it became that this gentle woman truly felt she would "hurt" her husband by telling him that he had an odor that could conquer Brooklyn. How could a good Christian wife do that? I suggested that she consider that there is a difference between hurt and injury.

"Let's imagine," I told her, "that I was a friend of yours and that without warning one evening I attacked you in a dark alley and stabbed you with a knife. You would wake up in the hospital with pain not only because of the stab wounds but also because I obviously meant you harm. You would ask yourself, *Why did Rich do this? What did he have in mind? What did I do to deserve such treatment?*

"On the other hand," I continued, "let's imagine I was a heart surgeon who, as your friend, noticed evidence of a serious heart condition, and, after tests confirmed that, you agreed to surgery. In that case you would wake up in the hospital with pain from where I cut you, but you would not feel injury. In fact, you would shake my hand, thank me for cutting you, and pay me a lot of money!"

Some pain can be constructive and is, in fact, inflicted with the intent of doing good. The Bible says, "Rebuke a wise man, and he will love you. Give instruction to a wise man, and he will be still wiser."[1]

That seemed to be a new concept to my caller, and she was relieved to have somebody suggest that it was okay for her to tell her husband how she felt. I have often wondered what happened at her house that night.

Disapproval Can Be Positive

Disapproval is not abnormal, it does not mean that a friendship or a marriage is diseased, and it is not un-Christian. In fact, serious conse- quences develop when people attempt to build a relationship without the effective expression of disapproval. Would you like to be the coach of a sports team that prohibited you from ever saying "You need to put some more practice into catch- ing the ball" or "Your pitching is falling off so I'm bringing in a relief man"? Would you want to be aboard an airplane whose pilot was never in- structed about his poor landings? Without any disapproval we will have an unrealistic and inac- curate view of ourselves.

Notice that I'm not talking about the heaping of guilt upon the heads of downtrodden people. I'm not encouraging unrestrained bursts of anger toward people who may have disappointed us. I am advocating sincere and effective expression, which does not intentionally cause injury but rather constructive good in the lives of the people we love. Disapproval is the factual information that helps a person who is seeking approval.

One of the effects of good communication is to help us resolve some of the feelings we have about others. Of course, our motive should not be one of dumping on another person, just so we can feel good at that person's expense.

I'll never forget a minor but humorous example of this. I had been invited to speak for a banquet in a city about an hour and a half from my home in southern California. My wife was going with me, so we asked another couple to join us.

It was mid-November and we were driving during the early evening, so it was beginning to get nippy outside. As we were cruising down the freeway, the husband lowered his window on the passenger side of the car. (We were in his car, but he had asked me to drive since I knew where we were going.) I thought to myself, *I guess he's the fresh-air type.* The cool wind felt good at first, but within a few minutes the interior of the car started getting cold.

My thought then was, *I wonder how long he's going to keep the window open and whether he's thinking about the two wives in the back seat. Aren't they getting cold?* After a few more miles, I saw my wife reach for her coat, and I started getting more impatient. *What a clod this guy is to have put down his window in such cool weather, without any apparent regard for his own wife, my wife, or me.* I couldn't believe it. Finally, I asked, "Would you mind putting your window up a bit?"

"Put the window up?" he asked. "You're the one who put it down. For the life of me I don't understand why!"

That turned my annoyance into embarrassment, and we quickly realized what had happened. His car had electric windows, all of which could be controlled from four buttons in the driver's door. I had accidentally hit the button for his window with my knee, and both of us had thought the other had decided to turn the car into an icebox. We had spent at least ten miles thinking identical thoughts about one another's insensitivity.

FEAR OF THE OTHER PERSON'S REACTION

Another obstacle hinders many of us from the effective expression of disapproval: our fear of the other person's reaction.

Each of us needs to evaluate whether or not we are allowing ourselves to be too intimidated by a person's reactions. This is important because sometimes another person's reaction is actually meant to protect that person from the pain of hearing the truth. Once we realize that, we might be more prepared to "punch through" the reaction and attempt to communicate.

Early in my marriage, Linda had a much clearer view of me in some areas than I did, especially when it came to my role as a father. Whenever she brought up the subject, I would try to listen to her in order to give the impression that I was a willing communicator. But the closer she got to the painful truth about me, the more uncomfortable I got. Eventually I would start using my inventory of devices designed to protect myself: I would get offended, I would get angry, I would try to remind her of some of her faults, and if all else failed, I would self-righteously grab my coat and say, "I'm going for a drive." Sometimes I even got her to feel guilty for trying to tell me the truth.

One fateful day, however, Linda finally got fed up with my antics.

We started the disagreement in the bedroom. It quickly escalated to an argument, and I managed to manipulate us in the direction of the family room, which gave me more space and put me within running distance of the front door. We finally ended up in the kitchen, and I used my final, and previously successful, tactic. "I'm going for a drive," I said, heading for the door.

"Oh no you don't," Linda said firmly. "I'm not going to let you do that this time. I've got something to say."

For the next ten minutes, she let me have it. She wasn't out of control and she wasn't abusive. She simply had something important to say and was not going to let me escape without her saying it.

My reaction, interestingly enough, was not one of anger. I was partly stunned at this new turn of events and partly amused. I had never seen Linda do this before, and I had to admit that she had "gotten" me. You see, what she didn't know is that in the past when I had gone out for my cooling-off drives, I had usually spent most of that time secretly feeling convicted about how right she was in what she had been trying to communicate. But I didn't want to admit it. This time she was not held back by the fear of my reactions, and I had to admit my wrong. Interestingly enough, we solved the whole issue within fifteen minutes.

Sometimes when counseling a couple, I'll ask, "Have you talked about this problem?" They'll say, "Oh, yes. Hundreds of times." As I look into their pattern of communicating, however, I will find that they may have approached the issue hundreds of times, but one person or the other successfully halted the communication before anything could be solved. Eventually they stop trying, blaming the other person's "reaction" for the failure.

Some people react violently to disapproval and that is a special problem. If you fear for your safety, then I understand your reluctance to express disapproval. Instead, you must reach out for help from people who have also experienced violence in their homes and are prepared to help you make decisions about your own safety. There are hotlines, shelters, special ministries at some churches, counseling centers, and law enforcement personnel who can help you, but only if you contact them.

A violent person is skilled at making other people feel as if they are the cause of his or her violence and that is frequently the reason their victims do not reach out for help. Don't allow yourself to go a moment longer believing that. There is *no* excuse for abusive and violent behavior, no matter how many faults and failures you may have in your life. Violence means that there is a serious problem in a home and someone from that home needs to be the person who finally says, "We need help." Nothing can be solved if you dodge the problem.

There is a risk to expressing disapproval. We need to choose the right time, the right way, and have the right motives. Sometimes we actually try to use disapproval to motivate others, which is a big mistake.

WHEN TO SPEAK

One anxious wife at a weekend marriage conference got so inspired about my discussion of disapproval that she went back to her motel room that evening and dumped twelve years of unexpressed bitterness on her husband all at once. As you can imagine, they ended up sleeping in different rooms.

She came to me the next morning and asked, "What happened? I thought my decision to finally express my disapproval was going to be the right thing?"

"Even if we come to understand the principles of love and approval and disapproval in a fresh way, we may not know how to apply them," I told her. Thankfully I was able to meet with this woman and her husband and reconcile the harm that was done.

I would like to suggest a principle to help us all exchange love, approval, and disapproval more effectively.

Doing Unto Others

In my opinion, one of the most valuable tools we can use for deciding what to do in relationships is given to us by Jesus Christ. We have somewhat tritely called it The Golden Rule, and in many of our minds it is nothing greater than a slogan printed on a bookmarker. Jesus, however, considered it the second most important concept that He taught, a rule of life, He said, that summarized God's law.

Jesus said, "Whatever you want men to do to you, do also to them."[2] In other words, if you and I are trying to decide how to relate to another person, we should use ourselves as a measuring stick for making that decision. How would we like to be treated if we were in that person's position?

I can't count the number of times I have asked the parents of teenagers, "Would you have responded to that kind of discipline when you were a teenager?"

The answer is usually, "No, I guess I wouldn't have!" Parents all over the globe have the fascinating tendency to treat their children and teenagers as they were treated when they were young, even if the treatment didn't work on them. We set aside the valuable input that could come from our own experience and treat other people in ways that our parents treated us.

Sandy was a young mother of two children. Almost from the beginning of her second marriage, she had felt uncomfortable with her new husband's mother. "I feel as if she's condemning me for the failure of my first marriage," she admitted. "How can I establish some peace between us? I want to love her and treat her right," Sandy said with tears in her eyes, "but I don't know what to do. I go to a family function where my mother-in-law is present, and I just become paralyzed."

My first conversation with Sandy occurred just before the Christmas holidays, so I suggested that she grit her teeth and get through the season as best as she could. I also asked her to keep a journal of what happened whenever she and her mother-in-law were together. After the first of the year, Sandy and I went through her journal carefully. We discussed several of the incidents in the journal and the ways Sandy had felt and responded at the time those events occurred. Then I asked Sandy, "If you were in your mother-in-law's place, how would you have responded?"

"I would have felt left out," Sandy replied.

"I wonder if, because of your concern over your mother-in-law's feelings, you haven't become so withdrawn and so silent in her presence that she wonders whether you like her at all?" I asked. "Based on what you've written in your journal, I'd say you arrive at family functions with your heart so prepared to be hurt by your mother-in-law that it is inevitable that she will hurt you, even if she does nothing."

I advised Sandy to put herself in her mother-in-law's place and to try to use that picture in her mind as a guide for her conduct.

Several weeks later Sandy shared with me some of what had happened. "One of the things I realized," Sandy said, "was that if I were my mother-in-law, I would want my daughter-in-law to show some evidence that she liked me at times other than just the family holiday gatherings. I began to identify with how good it would feel if my daughter-in-law unexpectedly dropped by my house with a basket full of home-baked cookies." Sandy then acted out that scenario, and although she did not stay at her mother-in-law's house for more than a few minutes, it helped her "connect" with the woman in a way that felt good. Later that night Sandy's mother-in-law called her to say how much she had appreciated the visit.

Some people have difficulty putting themselves in another person's place. It takes effort and, sometimes, almost a form of meditation, but it's worth it. Even if this measuring stick doesn't work all the time—even if the right treatment for us may not always be the right treatment for another—we avoid the hypocrisy of treating another person differently from the way we would want to be treated. Certainly we will be taking valuable steps in the right direction.

WHEN NOT TO SPEAK

A large percentage of the calls I receive on "Talk From the Heart" are about motivation: "How do I get another person to do what I want?" To illustrate, let me use a classic question: "How do I get my kids to clean their rooms?" This is what frequently happens:

I tell the kids to clean their rooms.

They either don't do it, or they do it so slowly that it will take a week to complete the job.

I remind them that the room needs to be clean, preferably before the end of this century.

They work more slowly.

I get mad and scream at them to get working.

They work even more slowly.

I threaten to put them on restriction.

They work so slowly I can hardly see them or they give up entirely.

I spank them.

I think to myself, *Why don't they obey? Do they really like being yelled at? It would be so easy if they would just quickly and easily do what I've asked.*

Sound familiar?

What frequently happens in this situation is that a parent starts using disapproval and punishment to motivate kids, but punishment does not motivate. We can write the truth in granite and post it at the doorway of our homes: *Punishment does not motivate.* We can't express disapproval to make people obey and rise to greater heights. Yet, many of us somehow imagine that if we pour on the disapproval and the threats and the punishment, other people will decide to do better.

Punishment, in my view, serves one very important purpose: it is the just reaction to conscious disobedience or defiance. If my child knowingly violates rules that have been clearly communicated, then that child should be punished. Punishment, when properly administered, is righteous and healthy. Punishment alone, however, does not motivate a person in the right direction. It merely holds that person accountable for having taken a wrong direction.

The motivator is approval. Approval communicates, "Well done, keep it up." Approval says, "You're on the right track." Approval inspires a person to take the next step toward a better performance. Do not express disapproval, as Elizabeth did, to motivate your children.

"I give up," Elizabeth, a young mother of three, told me one day when she called "Talk From the Heart." "I've tried everything and my kids still won't do their chores."

"What are some of the things you've tried?" I asked.

"I've asked them in nice ways and in not so nice ways; I've taken privileges away; I've spanked them; I've yelled at them; I've threatened to separate them from their friends. I've even tried paying them, but that didn't work either. How can I get them to do their chores?"

"In my opinion, young children like yours should first be introduced to chores on a small scale," I told Elizabeth. "A young child should be given the simple task of picking up a handful of toys or putting a few books back on the shelf. Whenever that is done satisfactorily, that child should receive simple approval from the parent, the communication of a job well done."

It is important that the child develop a reputation in his own eyes and in the eyes of the parents for being a good worker. Another fact to remember is that children love to imitate adults—they like to participate in what they see other people doing. How often, for example, have you seen the child who resists cleaning his room, begging to run the lawnmower or asking Dad if he can help wash the car? Sometimes the best introduction to chores is by working alongside of the child, always bearing in mind that the child needs to hear approval from your lips about the work that he or she does.

The same principle applies to places of employment and to marriages. Many marriages have come to ruin because of the belief of husbands or wives that the way to improve their mates is constantly to tell them what a poor job they are doing. Do you want your husband to come home on time? Communicate your approval when he does. Do you want your wife to prepare better meals? Give her something to look forward to when she does. Approval motivates.

"I can see that I've discouraged my kids and that they don't sense any of my approval," Elizabeth told me. "But what can I do now?"

"Even though I believe that the approval of a parent is the best motivation for a child," I replied, "sometimes that process needs a little help. I would suggest that you set up a reward system for your children. Allow them to earn points or prizes or money for their work. Put the responsibility on their shoulders, and you will establish a relationship in which you are rewarding them."

"I've tried something like that," she said. "It didn't work."

As Elizabeth and I talked about her reward system, I discovered that she had, indeed, let her children earn money for doing some of their work. For a couple of weeks they had seemed to like it, but their enthusiasm waned after that. Why? She required them to put all of the money in a bank, which may have seemed wise but didn't provide incentive for earning money, especially for a four-year-old.

"Unless they can use what they've earned for something they want, the system won't work," I told her. "Various parents have used reward systems, not just money. My wife, Linda, for example, has a closet full of goodies she calls The Grab Bag. At the end of the week the children get to go 'shopping' in The Grab Bag if their work for the week has been done satisfactorily."

Elizabeth decided to try a reward system. She set up a value for each chore, told the kids that every Monday evening would be "payday," and watched what happened. On the first Monday, the oldest daughter earned only a few pennies. The second daughter, who had done all of her chores, earned more than a dollar.

"I watched my oldest daughter's face that night," Elizabeth said, "and I saw her getting ready to say, 'Unfair.' It was really a revelation to her that there wasn't anyone in the entire room that she could blame. Under the old system, I was the culprit. She had blamed me for interrupting her fun to tell her to clean her room. She had blamed me for the punishment she got when she didn't clean the room. I couldn't win. This time, however, she had to carry the responsibility herself."

Elizabeth told me that the oldest daughter worked a lot harder the next week and that all three children eventually settled into doing their chores.

"The best part," Elizabeth said, "was that I got to hand them their money, and at the same time hand them my approval. The children and I really felt good about that."

There is a postscript to this story. Elizabeth's children are older now, and the reward system naturally faded somewhere along the way. The relationship of approval did not, however, and I think the reward system helped produce that.

Is it wrong to express disapproval? No. Is it wrong to express disapproval to motivate (your children or husband or wife)? Yes. Approval, not disapproval, inspires others to be the best they can be.

Chapter Six

"Won't I Make Matters Worse by Expressing Disapproval?"

One day a fifteen-year-old girl called me during a broadcast of "Talk From the Heart" to seek help in her relationship with her stepmother. From the beginning of their relationship, when the girl was ten, they had had problems. The daughter admitted that she had given her step-mom a lot to worry about, because she had been running around with the wrong crowd, had been caught drinking and experimenting with drugs, and was now having trouble with her school-work. "I feel like Mom just doesn't have time for me," the daughter said, "and that she is so angry about my problems that she doesn't want to talk about them."

I decided to zero in on the subject of communi-cation. Not surprisingly, most of the arguments in this girl's home started spontaneously. When they did, both she and her mom were so dedicated to defending themselves or dumping guilt on one another that nothing ever got settled.

I told her, "I'm going to guess that your stepmom loves you very much, and that she is just as frustrated about all of this as you are. She would be more willing to talk about it than you think." I suggested that she call her stepmom from school during the lunch hour and ask if they could get together that night for a coke at the local drive-in. "Don't tell your stepmom what you want to talk about, just ask her to get together with you," I warned.

Later the stepmom told me that she worried all afternoon about what the girl wanted to say to her. By the time they got together that night, the girl had thought through some of her problems with her stepmom and how they might be solved. What kind of a relationship could they have? She told her stepmother some of the changes she envisioned and was shocked when her stepmom, with tears in her eyes, said, "I'd love to have that kind of relationship with you. I've always thought that you didn't like me." They both, then, had the opportunity to express their areas of disapproval; although that caused some pain and some argument, they were no longer fighting against one another. They came away with the foundation for a whole new relationship.

I want to say clearly and emphatically that there are no guaranteed formulas for having a successful relationship with another person.

Even the best and the wisest of attempts to communicate love and approval or disapproval can fail miserably. The challenge is for each of us to discover ways to improve that kind of communication and to experiment with what will be most helpful to us. I'd like to share a few suggestions as a stimulation for thought.

1. DISAPPROVAL IS BEST EXPRESSED IN WORDS

Many of us think we are keeping the peace by keeping our mouths shut. The truth is, however, that our conduct is often a giveaway—what I smilingly refer to as "show and tell." If we don't "tell" another person about our feelings, we will "show" it in other ways.

I was introduced to this in a memorable way during my childhood.

Every neighborhood has an official grouch, a man or a woman who just seems to have been born in the objective case. In our neighborhood it was the lady who lived on the corner. Because I got along fine with most of the adults, it was confusing and irritating to me that this particular lady didn't seem to want my friendship. I didn't even like going past her house. There was always the danger that she was going to be at her door or on the front porch or—horror of all horrors—in her front garden, but even if you didn't see her, you could imagine a giant mist all around her house that seemed to say "I hate kids."

One Christmas I received a pair of new roller skates. I could hardly wait to spend some time on the sidewalks under a clear, blue southern California sky. I got about halfway down the block before I remembered that I would have to skate past her house. I avoided ever going that way except on my bicycle. If I rode fast enough, I might not see her, and if I did, it would only be for a second or two. The roller skates rendered me more vulnerable, I knew.

I decided to take the risk, and as I skated ahead, I wondered whether Christmas meant anything to her. Maybe she would not even be home.

A couple of houses before hers, I began to have trouble staying upright on my skates. The sidewalk was cracked and tilted a little. I didn't notice that she had come to the front of her driveway to pick up the morning newspaper. At almost the same moment that she leaned over to pick it up, I lost all control of my feet and crumpled into a dusty ball smack in front of her.

I was horrified. I had never been so close to her before. At first she looked at me with investigative concern to see if I was hurt. When it became obvious I was not, she broke into waves of giggles and described for me in detail how funny it had been to watch me progressively lose control. Instead of being embarrassed, I was amazed that this woman actually knew how to smile. She could talk to a kid without scowling.

As I unruffled my clothes and started to skate away, she said, "At least with the roller skates you won't be able to ride across the corner of my lawn like you do with your bicycle." It was said in a friendly way, but the significance of her words struck me with a blow.

She was right. I had made a practice of taking the short route around her corner by riding my bike on a small portion of her grass, not more than a couple of feet from the sidewalk. I had never thought it would cause any damage, but she had apparently begun to view me as a destructive pest who was dedicated to eliminating her greenery. Although she had never said anything, her irritation had been obvious. I just had never known why. I saw her a couple of days later, told her I was sorry for riding over her lawn, and vowed that it would not happen again. She was never unpleasant to me after that.

If we do not express our disapproval in words, we will instead use our actions, our inflections, our decisions, our lack of the expression of love. Not only does that not effectively communicate our feelings, but the other person also resents or misinterprets it, which makes the problem worse.

2. VERBAL DISAPPROVAL IS SOMETIMES BEST EXPRESSED IN WRITING

If my wife, Linda, and I get into an argument, I can use all kinds of clever devices to win it. That doesn't mean I'm right. It just means I win. One of the reasons is that I am more verbal than she is. I can dance around with words like a boxer in the ring.

One day Linda decided to write me a letter instead of getting into a personal confrontation. She gave it to me as I was going out the front door to an appointment. I was late, so I didn't have a chance to read the letter until noon. I remember laying out the contents of my sack lunch and grabbing the letter so I could munch and read at the same time. It was a new and disarming experience.

I got to the end of the first paragraph, where I would have interjected my objections, but I couldn't object. My wife wasn't there to intimidate. I had to let her written comments sit there and stare me in the face.

After reading the entire letter I was fuming. I set my lunch aside and constructed in my mind all the good responses to what she had written. I wished I could express them to her. After a while, however, I began to think about some of what she had said. By the time I got home that evening, not only had my anger subsided, but also I was willing to go to her, thank her for the letter, and ask her forgiveness for some of the problems. The roaring lion had been turned into a kitten because of the power of the written word.

One of the benefits of writing a letter is that we can express the whole range of what we're feeling. Arguments tend to focus on the negative, and our defensiveness is often based on the fear that we're being completely rejected. In a letter we can talk about how much we love a person— or how much we respect that person or how much we are committed to that person—as well as in what way we disapprove of the person.

3. DISAPPROVAL IS SOMETIMES BEST EXPRESSED BY PREARRANGEMENT

The vast majority of conflicts occur without warning. The disapproval may have been simmering for days or even for years but the actual exchanges just sort of "happen." However, when an important issue needs to be communicated to another person, it is sometimes best to plan an opportunity to talk about it.

I call this an "event of communication," in contrast to an ambush of another person.

I once counseled with Kathleen, the sister-in-law of a good friend of mine. She was weighed down with a whole range of concerns about her husband, Duane. He was working entirely too hard, she said, wasn't home very much, and, on top of that, was playing tennis two nights a week. She felt abandoned and feared that he would rather be anywhere but home with his family. She was also upset because some of the chores around the house were not getting done.

None of Kathleen's complaints was illegitimate, and I didn't sense she was exaggerating. The more we talked, however, the more I suspected that she was good at conducting "ambushes." She would spend the day letting her resentment build and then attack her husband when he got home or just after they had climbed into bed. He resented what he considered to be her uncooperative and unloving attitude, and that prevented him from hearing what she was trying to say. All of this, in turn, contributed to his desire to stay away from home. (He later admitted to me that he dreaded walking into the house, because he never knew when an ambush was going to take place.)

I told Kathleen she had nothing to lose by arranging an event of communication. "Try to back off on the ambushes," I suggested, "and have as calm a relationship with your husband as possible. Don't let your feelings interfere with dinner or making love or any other routine activities."

Then I suggested that she call her husband at work one day and ask to meet with him, because she had something important to talk over with him. I urged her to keep him in suspense about what she wanted to discuss.

Planning events of communication cuts down on ambushes, which are resented and, therefore, ineffective. Most family members have grown accustomed to when and where ambushes normally take place and are prepared to fend off the attacks. It's as though we develop an early warning radar to warn ourselves of the danger. If, for example, there has been a routine of arguments at bedtime, we'll approach bedtime with a great deal of caution, our defense systems armed and ready to fire in response to the slightest threat. At an event of communication, however, we can hopefully come to the peace table and agree to temporarily turn off the attack systems.

That's just what happened with Kathleen. About three weeks after we talked, she called to say that everything had gone beautifully. Her husband was so concerned when she called him that he agreed to take her out for dessert after dinner that night. (He later confessed that he thought she was pregnant or that she had decided to tell him she was leaving.) By the time they got to the restaurant, she had his undivided attention.

Kathleen started by apologizing for her tendency to ambush him. "I realize how difficult it must have been for you to live with my anger and frustration," she admitted. She then tried to explain what had caused her outbursts, particularly her fear about his never being home.

Because she admitted her mistakes to Duane, he was able to tell Kathleen that he knew he was a workaholic and needed her help to put life in the proper perspective. He also admitted that the more she fussed at him the more he intentionally stayed away from home. "But I do love you and the children very much," Duane assured her. "Can't we work together to change the situation?"

Kathleen went into their meeting prepared to

make a couple of suggestions as to how they might solve their problems, including counseling, and that was the beginning of their efforts to change their relationship.

Events of communication can occur in many different locations. You can go out for dinner, you can go for a walk, you can sit and talk at a park, you can go for a drive or spend the weekend at some far away place. The key is that you have both agreed to the event and both of you know that something important is going to be discussed.

One man who heard us talk about this on the radio called to say that his attempt to arrange such an event had failed miserably. I found out, through questioning him, that he had, indeed, invited his wife out for dinner and had prepared himself to talk about something of importance, but he had not told his wife about the purpose of the dinner. She thought they were going out for a nice evening on the town, and when he started setting the stage for what he wanted to communicate, she became furious. He had accidentally planned an ambush.

4. DISAPPROVAL IS BEST EXPRESSED WITH FACTS

Facts, rather than feelings, need to be used to communicate disapproval. Let's imagine that you hire a young man to be your gardener, but he does not do a good job. He doesn't rake the grass after mowing, he doesn't weed the garden, he doesn't trim the roses, and he fails to put the garden tools away after he is finished. You watch this happen week after week and you think to yourself, *Why doesn't this guy rake the lawn and weed the garden and do all the other things that good gardeners do?* Those are the facts. Because of those facts you are angry and you want him to change his behavior.

Instead, you may say to him, "You are a poor gardener. If you don't become a better gardener, I'm going to get someone else."

I'm sure you see, however, that your simply saying you are angry or telling someone else he is a failure is not completely effective. The person has no idea of what he or she has done wrong or how to improve.

Instead, the actual facts and consequences of a person's poor performance need to be communicated. It would be better to tell the gardener, "I expect the lawn to be raked, the garden to be weeded, the roses to be trimmed, and all the garden tools to be replaced. If those things are not done, then I will have to get another gardener." This places the facts before him and the responsibility more on his shoulders. And your words cannot be discounted by the person as subjective feelings. If he is truthful with himself, he will realize that he has not done these chores.

I received a call on the air from a weary wife who seemed ready to volunteer her husband for permanent duty aboard a space station. "My husband has a problem with spending too much money on too many unnecessary things," she said, "and that makes me very nervous. Too often I sound like a mother telling her son 'You shouldn't do that,'" she admitted.

She knew that he resented her attitude and felt it was his privilege, as the head of the household and the breadwinner, to spend the money any way he saw fit. Long and emotional arguments followed her disapproval of his irresponsibility.

After a few questions, I learned that she handled the budgeting, paid the bills, and wrote the checks. "You're in more of a position to know how much money the family has. . . . Instead of just telling him what a turkey he is, you need to tell him the facts of your family's finances."

She replied, "But he knows what our budget is. He knows how much we pay for rent and utilities and other bills. He just doesn't care."

"You need to make a simple accounting on paper," I told her, "and give it to him on a regular basis. If he wants to purchase something, just give him the facts and ask him to make the decision about where the rest of the money is going to come from." This wife didn't have to scream or cry or berate her husband's character. She did need to make sure that both she and her husband were operating on the basis of the same information.

Does this mean that feelings should never be expressed? No! Sometimes the feelings are the facts that need to be communicated. The important thing is to accurately describe the feelings and to communicate the facts about those feelings rather than dumping on the other person. It is better, for example, to say to your husband, "I'm so angry, I feel like hitting you," than to actually hit him. It is better to say, "I'm so depressed, I could jump off a cliff," than to actually do it.

I once talked with Rebecca, a young wife who was in a lot of pain because she wanted to have a baby but her husband wanted to wait. "We have been married seven years," she said, "and we originally agreed to have a family. But every time the subject comes up, my husband says he wants me to work for a few more years. He doesn't feel we're financially ready."

I wondered if her husband really knew how bitter and unhappy she was. If I asked him, "Do you realize how desperately your wife wants a baby?" would he answer, "Oh, it's not that bad. She's just a little emotional about it right now"?

I told this woman that she and her husband needed an event of communication. She agreed and asked him to go to one of their favorite spots on the beach the following Saturday to talk about something of great importance. (The husband later told me that he spent the rest of the week worrying about what she was going to say: he was so out of touch with her feelings that he never once thought about her desire to become pregnant.)

Once the couple arrived at the beach, Rebecca gave him a letter, which described all her feelings. She admitted desperation. She described a private fear that maybe God was actually suggesting that she would never have a child. The husband was aghast. She had never, even when they were planning their lives together, shared with him the depth of her desire to have children. She assumed he knew her desire and that he felt the same way himself. He, on the other hand, assumed that she understood what he considered to be their need to wait longer before having a family.

Feelings of desperation alone are not a good reason for making a decision, but this husband cared deeply about his wife and her feelings played a role in his own decision. It wasn't long before he agreed that it was time for them to begin to have a family.

5. THE MOTIVE FOR EXPRESSING YOUR DISAPPROVAL IS VITALLY IMPORTANT

Sometimes when we express disapproval to another person it is not our intention to try to solve anything. Our goal is to vent our anger and frustration or to make the other person feel guilty.

Before confronting another person, we need to think about what we hope to accomplish. If we want to come out of that event being able to hug the other person and say "I love you" or "I'm

sorry," then we're going to go into it differently
than if we expect to end the event by stomping
out the door or issuing a threat. Many of us think
only about the beginning of our communication
and how good it will be finally to let all the venom
come rushing out. We may go away with the satisfaction of having finally verbalized years of bitterness, but whatever relationship we had with
that person may actually have worsened or even
ended. The motive for the confrontation helps determine whether or not the confrontation should
take place at all and, if so, how it should take
place.

It is helpful to think of this in terms of execution versus rescue. The executioner approaches
the person with the problem, destroys that person, and then *walks away from* that person. The
rescuer approaches the person with the problem, addresses the person's problem, and then
walks away with the person.

6. EXPRESSION OF DISAPPROVAL SHOULD INCLUDE A SPECIFIC RECOMMENDATION ABOUT A SOLUTION OR THE PATH TOWARD A SOLUTION

Don't just tell somebody that there's a problem. Offer the beginning of a solution or make a
practical request.

Margie, a middle-aged woman with three children, came to me to talk about her husband, Don. He was a great guy, a gentle husband, and a kind father; he had been active in his church on an on-and-off basis. The problem was that he couldn't keep a job. From all appearances he was a capable person, and every new job seemed to promise permanence. But a few months later he would be unemployed again.

Margie had tried everything. She had scolded, cried, and threatened, but nothing had worked. She couldn't understand how Don, with all the financial pressure and personal embarrassment, could keep making the same mistakes.

I recommended to Margie that she arrange an event of communication with Don during which she express her love and commitment but also be honest about how difficult this had been for her and for the children, both financially and emotionally.

During their conversation Margie shared with Don that she had been thinking of leaving him but that she would like to stand beside him if he would take the additional step of getting help. She had located a professional counselor who specialized in helping people with career decisions and could help Don deal with the personal issues that were standing in the way of his keeping a job.

Don was receptive to the idea and, as far as I know, got the help he needed. It was the first time Margie had done something other than tell Don how serious their problems were, and it was the first time he had actually taken a step to try to find a solution. He had not been opposed to getting help, yet he had felt trapped in a cycle of failure.

We may feel inadequate to offer a solution, but often we can find help more easily than we might think. Let me mention a few sources I have found to be valuable:

Friendly Advice

The world is filled with people who have already walked the pathways we are now walking. Some of those people can help us immeasurably.

As a young husband and father, I thought I would never get ahead financially. I felt like a monetary dunce. I had a friend at the time who was about the same age as I but who never seemed to have any financial problems. *How did he do it?* I wondered. I finally decided to ask him to give me advice. I even swallowed my pride and opened all my financial records.

His advice was not what I expected. I was prepared for him to tell me to further tighten the belt, to eliminate even more from my budget, and to try to live on less income. Imagine my surprise when he said, "Rich, there's only one solution to this budget—and that's more money!" It prompted me to think about how I could grow financially and more adequately provide for the needs of my family.

Are your teen-agers causing you premature graying? Think about a person who seems to have things under control with his or her teen-agers. Ask for advice. Are you uncertain how to handle a dispute with your mate? Take the problem to somebody whose marriage you respect. Get advice to help you develop the skill of what to say and how and when to say it.

Advice from those who have walked the same paths that we are walking can be so valuable that organizations like Al-Anon, for the husbands and wives of alcoholics, have been formed to foster this communication. I always suggest these organizations to those with whom I counsel.

Books

Many times you can suggest or request that the other person read a book pertinent to the problem, or you can offer to read it together. There are self-help books on marriage, child rearing, sex, choosing a career, dealing with compulsive behavior, and almost anything else you're facing. In most communities there are Christian bookstores, which have a good selection of books on various subjects.

Churches

Most churches offer pastoral counseling, and some have other kinds of help available or know where you can get it. Your church can also be a valuable resource for laypersons who might be able to help in some specific area, such as employment or financial counseling.

Professional Counseling

A good professional counselor can help you save a lot of time in diagnosing and dealing with any problems in your life or in your family. The challenge, though, is to find a really good person. That can best be done through referrals from people you trust. If you have friends or family members who have had a good experience with a particular counselor or counseling clinic, ask them for a recommendation. Churches often have the names of professional counselors who are a part of their congregation or with whom they have a continuing relationship.

You don't have to wait until things are seriously wrong to consult a professional counselor. You can take that step any time you sense there is the need. It is of utmost importance, however, that you consult a professional counselor when certain conditions are in your life or in the lives of those around you, such as thoughts of suicide, violence in your home, or anything else that may be causing serious disruption.

Self-Help Organizations

If you can put a name to a problem in your life or in your home, there is probably a group of people in your community who have the same problem. It's important to decide whether you're experiencing alcoholism or satanic attacks or an eating disorder or a drug addiction or the results of losing someone in death or the effects of a divorce. Getting together with others who have special knowledge of your condition can be invaluable.

A DRAMATIC EXAMPLE
OF SUCCESSFUL
CONFRONTATION

Although some Christians fear that confrontation is not spiritual and believe that the pain of it is to be avoided, they might be surprised to learn that one of the most sensational and successful techniques of confrontation is patterned after the teachings of Christ. Jesus said that if somebody sins against you, confront that person. If that confrontation doesn't accomplish anything, then take two or three others with you to confront the person. Frequently, this confrontation will solve the problem. If not, Jesus said, take the matter to the entire church.

Jesus knew the power of a person's being confronted either by an individual or by a group. I'd like to tell you about the technique inspired by this teaching, not because everyone should use it in every situation, but because it contains the essential ingredients of effective confrontation. However, this method is always used under the direction of trained professionals and only in response to chronic problems in a person's life.

The technique is called *intervention* and was popularized by an Episcopal priest who had been an alcoholic and who had felt that there must be a way to intervene in the downward spiral of other alcoholics, instead of waiting for them to reach bottom. Intervention is now used by professional alcoholism counselors throughout the United States and in some other parts of the world, and I am among those who are encouraging its use for other serious conditions, such as violence in the home, eating disorders, and other kinds of substance abuse.

The results of intervention are astonishing. More than 90 percent of even the most hardened alcoholics come out of the intervention agreeing to seek help for their problem. One of the counselors with whom I have spent a great deal of time has been leading interventions for more than eight years and has never seen a failure. When you're talking about such a widespread and frustrating problem as alcoholism, that's a remarkable success rate.

Intervention begins with family members and friends of the alcoholic. They meet with the counselor to receive help identifying in factual but nonjudgmental ways what kind of pain has been caused each of them by the alcoholic. They learn to put their pain into words, and in some cases, memorize what they will say to the alcoholic at the proper time so it will be effective.

Then, one evening when the alcoholic arrives home from work, for example, he finds all of the people who mean the most to him gathered in his living room—his wife, his children, his pastor, his brother, and his best friend. The intervention counselor is there as well. He introduces himself or herself to the alcoholic, briefly describes what is about to happen, and what the consequences will be if the alcoholic chooses not to listen.

Then, one by one, each person in the room shares what he or she has been trained to say. The presentations are from the family's and friends' hearts and experiences, but they have been put into terms that are factual, noncondemning, and usually very painful to the alcoholic. Next, the intervention counselor communicates the family's request—such as, that the individual immediately enter a treatment program—and also explains the consequences if he does not comply. Frequently, the consequence is that the wife and any children in the home are going to go live with someone else for a while. They will not return until the alcoholic agrees to enter treatment. In almost every case the alcoholic agrees, and sometimes a car is actually waiting to take him to enter a treatment center.

Are you ready for the clincher? The average professional intervention takes less than ten minutes! Many of them are only five or six minutes. It's hard to believe that a problem, which may have plagued a family for a lifetime and which family members have tried in vain to change, can be confronted so successfully in just a few minutes.

Intervention works because of several factors. It includes people who are important to the alcoholic and who agree that his drinking is a serious problem; it includes a noncondemning, non-judgmental communication of the facts about his problem; it contains a specific solution to the problem; it includes a consequence if he chooses not to get help.

Let me say it again: Intervention should not be attempted without the help of those who have been trained to do it right. I've known people who have tried intervention on their own and ended up with a room full of people who spend two or three hours arguing with one another and accomplishing nothing.

In this chapter I have tried to cover some helpful information about effective disapproval. There is no guarantee that any particular technique or device will produce any particular results. The challenge is to learn the skills and pursue the paths that may be helpful to you and to those whom you love.

PART FOUR

Self-Image

Chapter Seven

"How Do You See Yourself?"

Almost every day on "Talk From the Heart" callers refer to self-esteem. A mother calls and says, "My son is having trouble at school, and I think his self-esteem is really low." A young woman mentions, "My counselor says my problem is I don't love myself." A man who says he's going through mid-life crisis complains, "I've never had good self-esteem."

Twenty-five years ago when I first heard the term *self-image,* an aged psychology professor was teaching the concept in a manner that was as dusty and academic as the classroom setting. Now terms like *self-esteem* and *self-concept* are among the buzz words of the day. Still, any discussion about feelings and relationships will inevitably include our feelings about ourselves.

For some, the subject of self-image is a controversial one and I understand why. We are living during a time when "me" and "what is important to me" seem to be the ultimate values of the appropriately named "me generation."

SELF-LOVE

The prevailing doctrine right now seems to be "self-love." The theory is that somewhere along the path of life I have lost my natural love for myself and now I have to get it back. Volumes of books and hundreds of seminars are designed to do just that. For instance, a friend of mine attended a weekend event during which he and others spent secluded hours chanting positive phrases like, "I love myself and will treat myself in loving ways today." These slogans were designed to help the participants renew their love affair with themselves. He said it worked—for a while.

I don't agree with the self-love movement, but I'm not overly critical of it either. I think it has arisen because of a real and observable need in our lives and has offered thousands of people some temporary relief from personal pain. However, I don't think it addresses the depth of what each of us hungers for, and it is just a matter of time before people realize that.

John, a radio colleague of mine, telephoned me one day with some concerns about his girlfriend. "I'm not very religious," he told me, "but I'm really concerned about this group that Jennifer's been attending, and I don't know whether it's good or bad for her."

I arranged to meet Jennifer and discovered that she was an attractive and intelligent person who had suffered from depression most of her life and carried a lot of pain in her heart. She had been attending weekend meetings sponsored by an organization that promised her a new life of loving and living. "We heard a lot of lectures saying that God didn't exist and that if we tried to believe in Him and rely on Him, we were weak," she told me. "We spent hours meditating on ourselves and our abilities and our potential and being told that if anything good was going to happen in life, it would be because we learned to love ourselves."

At first, Jennifer was virtually intoxicated with the seminars. She returned to work with a new zeal that was noticed by her co-workers. John told me that he was also quite amazed by the apparent change in her feelings about herself. The only problem was that John didn't think the change was real or permanent. "Jennifer seems to be on a high," he told me, "but she is also in her own little world. Not only that but she has started living in a form of denial."

The seminar had taught her, for example, that there was no such thing as sin or personal failure and that she shouldn't think about such things. During this time her performance in her sales profession fell, but she refused to admit it. Eventually Jennifer came to a crisis point where her job was in jeopardy and her relationship with her boyfriend was disintegrating. Finally she realized that the seminars had only introduced her to a very intense and contrived world, which didn't include reality.

I had the privilege of helping Jennifer in two significant ways. First, she came to realize that the root of her depression and her awful feelings about herself came from her childhood experiences as a victim of incest. Children who have been molested often feel responsible for the molestation. Jennifer's feeling of responsibility and of being bad for having sexual experiences with an adult made Jennifer feel an overpowering guilt. The seminars had encouraged her to pretend as though the pain was not there and to build her life on positive phrases and principles. What she actually needed was to walk in the direction of the pain and resolve it. That would require a season of professional counseling in her life.

The second important thing that happened in Jennifer's life was that she came to know God's love and His forgiveness through Jesus Christ's death on the cross. Christ's sacrifice for her and the love it demonstrated had more impact on her than her trying to discover love for herself.

SELF-IMAGE

One of the ways to distinguish self-love from a natural respect of one's God-given talents and abilities is to return to my psychology professor's terminology. I prefer to talk in terms of *self-image* as opposed to *self-love* or *self-esteem*.

Self-image is simply the view I have of myself. This word doesn't suggest love or hate, high or low, good or bad.

The goal for each of us, I believe, is to have an accurate self-image—to see ourselves the way we really are and to live life based on this reality.

Unfortunately, we all know persons who are not able to do this. Many of us have spent time trying to convince someone who feels lousy, but is in fact quite talented, to appreciate his or her ability. A good-looking person is often convinced he or she looks like a mold experiment. We've all struggled with feelings of inadequacy or with the fear that we don't fit in.

The solution is to step back and take an honest look at ourselves, at the people around us, and at some of the conditions that have helped form our views of ourselves. After all, some of the negative feelings people wrestle with are valid. I believe we have been created to feel inadequate for all the times that we are, in truth, inadequate.

If you asked me to pilot a Boeing 747 jetliner, you would be inviting me to fill a role for which I am not qualified. I do not know how to fly a Boeing 747, even though I am certified to fly smaller planes like Cessnas and Pipers. My feelings of inadequacy, then, would be appropriate, and my image of myself would be true. I would tell you, "No, I will not accept your invitation to be the pilot of that airplane because I know nothing about

how to fly it." My accurate self-image would pre-
vent the loss of my own life and many others.

False Inadequacy

When our fear or guilt or feeling of inadequacy
does not correspond to reality, we experience
false guilt, needless fear, a fruitless feeling of inadequacy.

Ashley was a classic example of this. "My husband is being unfaithful to me," she said. "He is
having an affair with one of his old girlfriends."

I might have believed that except the person
who had recommended me to Ashley had told
me that Ashley's husband was devoted to her
and had never cheated on her.

"What makes you think your husband is having an affair?" I asked.

"He denies it," she replied, "but I know that he
sees her because they are in the same professional association and attend some of the same
meetings. He also comes home late a lot."

As I counseled with Ashley, the picture became clear. She had had a very painful childhood, during which she experienced the sudden
and tragic loss of her father in a fatal traffic acci-
dent. Because of her experiences, she viewed
herself as deserving to lose the people who
meant the most to her. Although her husband
wasn't an adulterer, she felt that she was eligible
to lose him—a fear based on an unreal view of
herself.

Misleading Feelings

Many of us have never made the distinction between facts and feelings, or realized that sometimes feelings can exist without any factual basis. For example, we've all gone through frightening circumstances, such as getting lost in a department store as a child or being confronted by a fierce dog or experiencing some natural disaster like an earthquake or a tornado. The feelings that accompany those experiences are unforgettably real; thus, it's easy to conclude that those feelings are always founded on reality. Unfortunately, we make the mistake of living and making choices based on that assumption.

I'll never forget a night I spent as a child in an isolated mountain cabin. I was convinced there was a bear on the front porch. I didn't see any bear or have any other hard evidence that a bear was there, but some of the noises I heard and the shadows I saw through the window scared me to death. For about an hour I worried about dozens of questions. I was sleeping on an enclosed portion of the porch and wondered whether or not I could safely open the door to the cabin and get inside with my parents without the bear noticing. If he came after me, what should I do? Lie still? Scream?

The noises finally stopped and I drifted off to sleep, but the next morning I scoured the front yard of the cabin looking for bear tracks. I never found any, but I did discover that my "bear" was the limb of a tree, which had been scratching against the porch and casting eerie shadows in the moonlight.

We need to realize that feelings, no matter how real they seem, can sometimes be feeding on the wrong information. When that happens, we can't afford to respond to the feelings without investigating the facts and evaluating what produced the feelings. We must get in touch with what's true—even if that may not be particularly positive or encouraging.

WHAT PRODUCED THE FEELINGS?

At the root of many of our personal problems is a reality that's not very pretty and sometimes hard to face, such as Jennifer's discovery that she was a victim of incest or Ashley's having to resolve a painful childhood that included the loss of her father. Both Jennifer and Ashley had spent their lives not wanting to face their pain; therefore, they were not able to resolve their feelings.

If we're pretending that a painful past didn't occur, we are setting ourselves up for two unfortunate conditions. First, we will not have an accurate self-image because we don't want to deal with the truth. Therefore, our feelings and choices will be based on lies. Second, we will be classic candidates for the self-love movement, which often encourages people to ignore the painful truth and to dedicate themselves to thinking positive and happy thoughts, even if they do not correspond with reality.

You might ask, "Are you in favor of positive thinking and meditating on good things?" My answer is "Yes," but only when the lies in a person's life have been openly addressed and some of the wounds have been healed. Many teachers and followers in the self-love and positive thinking movements are placing layers and layers of fine-sounding concepts on top of diseased and hurting people. They are simply bandaging over wounds, which keep on bleeding, even though everybody pretends the wounds are not there.

THE TWO PARTS OF SELF-IMAGE

I view self-image as having two halves, which are separate yet similar. These parts are distinct, yet together they make the whole that is you or me:

1. The "who I am" part of self-image
2. The "what I do" part of self-image

My view of myself can be summarized in terms of being and doing.

From the time that I am born I am asking "Who am I?" and "How am I doing?" I am constantly gathering information about myself. Every new experience adds to my collection— every glance, every word that is spoken, every success, every failure, every comparison that is made between me and someone else.

The "who I am" part of self-image is formed and nourished by love. Love, as we've already defined it, is anything that I do for someone because of who that person is. It is not earned. It is a gift by choice on the part of the giver. It addresses our hunger to know "who I am" as opposed to "what I do." Without genuine, distinct expressions of love, at least half of my self-image is going to be malnourished.

The "what I do" part of self-image is formed and nourished by approval and disapproval. My hunger to perform in ways that fit in—in ways that grant me the confidence of achieving to the satisfaction of those around me—is fed by good feedback.

It is vital that both halves of my self-image be constructed and sustained by that which is truthful. It won't do any good for me to imagine that I am loved by somebody who does not love me. It will be harmful if I pretend that I'm doing a good job when, in fact, I'm not. It will be devastating if some of the feedback I get is not honest or accurate, as happened to a young man I counseled.

One Sunday after the morning service I was approached by this young man who was visiting our church for the first time. I had noticed him sitting in the congregation because he wore an unusually large pair of dark glasses and was dressed in odd, multicolored clothes. I had never seen or met this man before; yet, he came to me and said, "Why are you ignoring me?"

My answer was quite blunt, but I've learned to immediately correct a misstatement. "Let's get something straight right now," I replied. "I don't know who you are, I don't remember ever meeting you, and I am not ignoring you."

"Oh," he replied with a bit of a blush. "I guess I had the wrong impression."

He said that his name was Charles and that he had a lot of questions about religion. "Can we get together sometime and talk?" he asked. I was kind of intrigued with the guy, and we agreed to meet during the week.

Charlie, as I called him, turned out to be one of a kind. He was deeply involved in the occult, had been in and out of dozens of churches, was living the life of a virtual recluse, and, in my opinion, had some deep emotional problems. Yet, I liked Charlie. He was very intelligent, had a unique and appealing sense of humor, and a sincere interest in his spiritual life.

I counseled with Charlie often in the following months and the story that emerged about his life was a horror. It was best illustrated by a telephone conversation I overheard between him and his mother:

"Hi, Mom, this is Charlie."

"Why are you calling? Don't you know how much it affects my heart condition when you call? You're a mess. I don't want to ever hear from you again."

"I'm calling to say I love you, Mom. I just wanted to know how you are feeling."

"Just go away and leave me alone. You make me sick. I don't even like hearing your voice."

Charlie's mother had treated him like that for his entire life. As a boy, Charlie had been locked in closets, violently beaten, and at times, literally thrown out of the home. One particularly painful incident occurred when he was eight years old. His mother got angry with him about something, stormed into his room, and spent about fifteen minutes throwing all of Charlie's possessions out of a second-story window. She would not allow him to go down and retrieve any of them.

Another day, during a fit of rage, Charlie's mother broke the news to him that he was adopted. She made the story sound as pitiful and black as she could and purposely tried to make Charlie feel that it was his fault that his natural mother had given him up for adoption—even though he had been relinquished at birth. She told Charlie he was Korean, then talked about how much she hated Koreans.

I have been deeply involved in the lives of adopted persons and their families because I am adopted myself. I recommended to Charlie that as a part of his counseling, he look into his biological roots and find out more about his birth background. Charlie was from a state which freely shared adoption information and everything he wanted to know came a couple of weeks later in a letter from the county where he was born. Nothing his mother had told him was true. His natural mother had relinquished him for adoption because she felt that was the best decision for Charlie. It had actually been an act of love. She had made that choice not only for Charlie, but also for his *twin brother*. That's right! We discovered Charlie had a twin brother. Additionally, Charlie was not part Korean, as he had been led to believe, but was almost full-blooded American Indian.

Charlie has spent many years learning more and more truth about himself and along with that has come amazing change. He is no longer a recluse. He has come to accept God's love for him and is slowly reconciling some of the distortion from his past.

I had the privilege of performing Charlie's wedding, and he is now living in a part of the country that is nearer his twin brother and other members of his birth family. He will forever remain in my memory as one of the most dramatic examples of what can happen when a person gets unreal and inaccurate feedback about himself from some of the people who are helping to form his self-image.

How do we correct and adjust an inaccurate self-image? By allowing something which we almost instinctively resist: honest comment from the people around us. Author Gary Smalley says, for example, that most of us men don't have to go outside our homes to learn how to be better husbands; all we have to do is consult our wives. He says a wife is the best marriage manual available!

What he is saying is that husbands and wives probably have a more accurate assessment of each other than they do of themselves. In order to develop a more realistic self-image, we must be willing to talk with the people who know us best or with others who are in the position to give us accurate feedback. My friend Charlie, of course, couldn't get that kind of help from his mother because she was the one who had a warped view of life and was responsible for a lot of the lies he believed about himself. That happens occasionally and when it does, we need to look elsewhere for help. If your view of yourself is being primarily affected by a person who has a lot of problems, you need to realize that and identify the people in your life who can help you the best.

SELF-IMAGE IS BASED ON WORTH

The questions of "Who am I?" and "How am I doing?" are not the result of a simple quest for data. Our hunger for worth is the reason we are concerned with our self-image. What value is there to the fact that I exist? To whom am I valuable and why? What can I do to improve my value?

When I counseled with Jennifer, the girl who had attended the self-love seminars, she spent one of our sessions talking about her search for love and self-worth.

"Love seemed elusive to me," Jennifer told me. "I wondered if I had ever truly experienced love. I didn't feel that my father loved me. I didn't remember any love from my brother and two sisters. My mother had severe psychological problems, so I never expected to receive love from her. I didn't even feel like my boyfriend loved me. I just felt bankrupt when it came to love."

At the seminars Jennifer and other love-seekers were instructed how to meditate on loving themselves. They were given plaques to hang on the walls at home or to tack to the refrigerator door. The plaques had slogans such as, Do yourself a favor. Love yourself today, and If you don't love you, you cannot love anyone else. It wasn't until several months had gone by that Jennifer was able to admit that she didn't really feel much better about herself. Her hunger for her father's love was just as intense as it had ever been. She still had difficulty believing that her boyfriend really loved her. She came to realize that her need was not to love herself, but was to be loved by others. During the times when she meditated alone in the mountains, she experienced some emotional highs, but when she came back to the people who meant the most to her, she felt the same insecurities and hindrances to love. "I remember saying to myself once," she reflected, "that I wish my father were attending a seminar where he would be required to meditate on and increase his love for me."

What Is Your Value?

Jennifer's story introduces a very important fact of life and of self-image: Each of us wants to be of value to somebody else. To put it another way, each of us wants to be worth something to another person.

Jennifer discovered that in order to have worth, "we have to be worth something to somebody else." Sitting in a room alone chanting phrases to ourselves doesn't address that hunger. We want to know what phrases are being said about us by other people. Gold wouldn't be worth anything if people didn't consider it valuable. In fact, other cultures in the world use items like sea shells or stones or even animal bones for currency. It's the same with human worth.

Worth is assigned to us by those who are most important to us. We can try to imagine that we are immune from this if we wish, but it's not likely that anyone is.

Falling in love, for example, is an especially intense way of evaluating worth. Can you remember coming home from your first date with somebody and hating yourself for half the things you said? Why? Because you were afraid it was going to affect that person's decision to value you. Your value of yourself at that moment meant nothing. You wanted your date to value you.

All of this is of enormous importance because the choices we make in life, both big and small, are based on our view of ourselves and on our assessment of our worth, more so than most of us realize.

I'll never forget a sorrowing mother who came to talk with me about her sixteen-year-old daughter, Sharon.

"I'm worried sick," the mother cried, "because she's fallen in love with a twenty-two-year-old high school dropout who is an alcoholic and who occasionally mistreats her. And yet she sticks with him. I just don't understand it." The mother said this relationship had existed for more than a year, despite her attempts to discourage it.

The ironic part of the story was that Sharon's father was an alcoholic and had mistreated her, too. The mother could not understand why her daughter would choose to get into the very same kind of relationship that had already caused her so much pain.

I met with Sharon and her mom together before referring both of them to a professional counselor. Their situation became clearer as we talked. First, Sharon should never have had to experience the abuse at the hands of her father. Somebody, most notably Mom, should have blown the whistle a long time ago and gotten help for herself and her daughter. That had not happened, however, and now there were gaping wounds in both of them, which would require professional help to address.

Second, Sharon's choice to commit herself to this unlikely boyfriend was explained by a lot of factors, not the least of which was her self-image and the assessment of worth that resulted from it. For sake of this discussion let me use the common "0–10" way of rating things, 0 being the worst and 10 being the best.

From all appearances Sharon had a lot going for her. She was very attractive, for example, easily rating an 8 in anybody's book. She was a straight-A student, which would rank her a 10 academically. She had a lot of friends and was a cheerleader, which would give her at least an 8 or a 9 in the popularity department. In those and a lot of other ways she was a fine girl.

She could have had her pick of many of the boys on campus but instead had chosen to love a very needy man who had little to offer her and who, as her mother reported, actually mistreated her. One of the biggest reasons for her choice was that the boyfriend's treatment of her matched her own feelings of what she was worth.

Sharon's classmates, friends, and teachers may have valued her as an 8 but her home, particularly her father, had treated her like a zero and her own evaluation of herself was probably a 1 or a 2. Her self-image was blurred and marred, and she was making her choices on the basis of what she estimated her value to be. I can imagine that she felt that some of the finest boys on campus, many of whom had tried to romance her, simply outclassed her.

Children of abuse and alcoholism are affected by a lot of other factors, too. They have been hurt so they tend to become rescuers. They also enter into life with such a hole in their hearts for a father's or mother's or anybody's love, that they are willing to pay high prices to fill that void. They have so lost their ability to fight against mistreatment without feeling guilt, they become prey for others who need to overpower someone.

But at the heart of their pain is a crippled

sense of worth, a feeling that whatever they're going through is somehow what they deserve and they can't conceive of their making any different choices.

Self-image is important not only because of our need for worth and to assess "who I am" and "what I do," but also because we base all the decisions and choices of life on our self-image and our self-worth. If these choices are based on lies, we have little chance to fulfill our true potential.

Chapter Eight

"Have You Felt God's Love?"

Jesse was one of those special people you meet along the pathway of life and know you will never forget. She came into our lives during the early years of our ministry, when I was the associate pastor of a church in central California. Even though the church wasn't large, Jesse could be virtually invisible. She was a pleasant but plain-looking person who sat toward the rear in Sunday services where she would not be noticed.

My first memory of Jesse was when she sheepishly walked toward the front of the sanctuary after a Sunday evening service and quietly said she wanted to ask a question. Her voice trembled and her eyes wouldn't make contact with mine. She seemed terrified. Her question was powerful in its simplicity. She asked, "How do I get to know God?"

Jesse and I counseled numerous times over the following weeks and the more of her story I learned, the more I was astonished that she was alive and functioning at all.

"My family was not a close one," she told me. "My father was gone most of the time, working in the oil fields of Oklahoma, and my mother hated me. I had an older brother but he joined Mom in mistreating me." Jesse's story was one of repeated abuse. When her father was at home, he demanded sex from her. When the father was not home, her mother would lock Jesse in a tiny, windowless room for days at a time, threatening her so she would not tell anyone. Her brother sexually molested her as well.

"I began to fantasize," she continued, "and that fantasy world became the world where I lived. Instead of being in a dark closet, I could be in a foreign country or the daughter of some important person who loved me." Jesse somehow made it into adulthood and as is often the case with a person who has experienced abuse, she married a person who was an abuser. Happily, he became a Christian and sought help for his problems. Her question "How do I get to know God?" came from a deep hunger of not only wanting to know God's love but wanting to know anybody's love. I referred her to a counselor who had specialized knowledge of abuse.

There were a lot of exciting breakthroughs, but the most significant one came about three months after she started counseling. She had been going through the painful, but necessary, process of facing exactly what had happened to her in her childhood and calling it what it was—abuse. She had carried the guilt of what happened to her and, like many victims of abuse, actually thought it was all her fault.

"God's love for you is unconditional, Jesse," I told her. "That means there isn't anything you can do to earn it and nothing you can do to lose it. He loves you because of who you are. In fact," I continued, "He says that it was while we were sinners, while we were in rebellion against Him and disobeying Him, that He looked upon us with love and compassion and sent Jesus to be our Savior. God didn't say, 'You'd better become perfect so I can love you.' He said, 'I already love you and I know you'll never be perfect so I'll send Jesus to pay for all your imperfections and then I can have relationship with you.'"

Jesse was awed. "I have spent my life trying to overcome my problems," she said, "and trying to be good so I could have love. All the people in my life have required that. If I'm not good, I don't feel that I deserve their love."

"One of the most damaging results of confusing love and approval," I told her, "is that we will tend to relate to God the same way as we relate to people. We will think He is requiring us to perform in order to receive His love. When we fail and when we are obviously not perfect, we won't feel eligible for His love."

I suggested that she spend the next several days really thinking about this. "The Bible says we should actually meditate on God's truth," I admonished. "The word in the Bible for *meditate* suggests the action of a cow's chewing her cud. We chew on the truth over and over and over again. God loves you just the way you are and wants to help you overcome some of the pain in your life."

A couple of Sundays later I was sitting on the platform in the sanctuary, preparing to start the morning service. I glanced out over the congregation. You could see Jesse a mile away. She was sitting in her usual spot, toward the back, but she was beaming like a lighthouse. She sang the songs with joy and animation and wiped her eyes from time to time. I knew something had happened. I couldn't wait until I saw her after the service. She told me her story before I even commented on the change in her appearance.

"I was at a laundromat last Tuesday morning," she said. "I had been thinking about God's love night and day for almost a week. Suddenly, while sitting in the laundromat waiting for the clothes to dry, it hit me. God loves me! I am loved by somebody! I am loved by the most important Person in my life!" She said she softly prayed, thanking God for His love and telling Him that she was going to trust that Christ had actually paid the price for her imperfections. She told God that she realized that Christ did this because of His unconditional love that nothing could hinder. "A warmth came over me and I felt such an eruption of joy in my heart that I thought to myself, *I'm going to make a scene right here in the laundromat.*" Jesse said the only thing she could think of to do was head for the restroom where she locked the door, turned on both water faucets to dampen the noise, and let the joy gush from deep within.

Like many others I had counseled, Jesse had sought help from the self-love movement years earlier. "Years ago I bought a book which promised to help me love myself," she once told me. "Because I lived in a private, fantasy world anyway, I thought I could succeed." It was the experience of knowing God's love, however, that made her realize why the self-love project didn't work. She wasn't hungry to love herself. She was hungry to be loved. Her fantasy world was one of her own making, and even if she sometimes felt pretty good in that world, there was always the reminder that those who were around her and the most important to her did not love her. "Now, I sometimes walk through the aisles of the grocery store saying to myself, *I am loved,*" she said. "It's unbelievable to me."

Jesse's experience illustrates the most important truth about love. Not only do we instinctively hunger for love but we instinctively hunger for the love of Him who created us: God. No human love is ever going to fill perfectly what God intended to be filled by His love alone. Knowing that we mean something to the most important Person in existence will change our whole sense of being.

Think about it with me. God loves you.

His love is without any strings attached. Unconditional. You don't have to do a single thing to earn it. In fact, as a human being you can't possibly earn it. You cannot lose His love. Nothing you have ever done or could ever do would accomplish that. If you could lose it, then what He offered you could not properly be called love.

When you feel like a failure, He loves you. When you sin, He loves you. When you feel ugly, He loves you. When you feel out of place, He loves you. When you experience loss, He loves you.

It is God's love, not self-love, that feeds the deepest cravings of the heart. The "who I am" part of myself does not cry out for me to mean something to me or for me to have worth to me. Standing under the night sky and saying, "I love me" really means very little. No, the declaration that penetrates the darkness to echo through the heavens is one that comes from the overflowing spirit of a tiny human being who can stand with a confident heart and uplifted arms and cry, "I AM LOVED BY THE ALMIGHTY GOD!"

DIVINE LOVE

The early Christians called this unconditional love, *divine love,* which distinguished it from anything else they had ever known. They even used a different word in their Greek language to describe it, the word *agape.* They had words for the love between friends and the love between lovers. But God's love was in a different category. Even though we can feel and experience God's love, His love goes beyond feeling. One person has said, "Probably the closest human example of the kind of love God has for us is the love that a married person would have for a mate who is in a lifeless coma." Divine love cares without depending on anything in return. It is a love that can certainly produce feelings, and it's nice when the feelings are there, but it's also a love you can count on regardless of whether or not you feel it.

GOD'S LANGUAGE OF LOVE

We've talked about the importance of knowing a person's language of love. What is God's language of love? How does He express His love so that we may know it? In my opinion, a lot of us have expected God to communicate His love in ways that are based on our expectations rather than on His truth.

Paul was a successful businessman whom I had occasion to talk with from time to time. One day during lunch he said, "I'm really having a hard time spiritually right now. I feel distant from God and feel that He doesn't love me."

"How does God express His love to you?" I asked.

Paul was thoughtful for a moment, then said, "I guess I've never thought about it."

Our conversation revealed that Paul was relating to God on the basis of approval. He confessed that he had been toying with the idea of having an affair with a woman who worked for him. Also, one of his businesses was going through a rough time, and he was considering filing for bankruptcy. I helped him realize that his guilt over the relationship with his female friend was partly responsible for his feeling distant from God.

"Not only are you facing true guilt," I told him, "but you also are believing that as long as you sin, God doesn't love you. In other words, you are feeling that as long as you fail to perform correctly, God removes His love from you. That's worse than the guilt because it's a lie. Additionally," I continued, "you are interpreting the business failure as evidence that God doesn't love you. You seem to consider success to be evidence of God's love and failure to be evidence of the absence of His love."

Paul quickly admitted that my observations were right. "How *does* God express His love to me, then?" he asked.

"There are several ways," I replied, "but the most important is one which many of us are familiar with yet have failed to recognize." I reminded Paul of the writings of the apostle John, a man who was a close friend of Jesus. John wrote about love more than any other writer of Scripture and he once defined God's love.

"This is love," he wrote, "not that we loved God . . ." It's important that each of us really listens to those first words. Because of our guilt, many of us feel that any lack of love between us and God is our fault and that we have failed to love Him enough. I've even seen some well-meaning books which have urged Christians to focus on their love for God and to try to increase or improve it.

But John says, "This is love: not that we loved God, but that He loved us and sent his Son as an atoning sacrifice for our sins."[1] John is saying that Jesus is God's language of love.

Sometimes I wish we could hear the story of Jesus as though for the first time. As the story begins, we would hear about a Person who is God and who emptied Himself in such a way that He came to live among us. He was perfect and didn't have any sin of His own, which would have required Him to die. Yet this Person innocently went through torture, humiliation, and death on our behalf. He paid the price—death—required for our sin. And there isn't any good explanation for it except love. God's most powerful and effective expression of His love is Jesus, and people experience changed lives when they come to realize that.

"So that is the most important way God expresses His love to us," I told Paul. "He says He loves us and proves it by what Jesus did.

"There are other ways He expresses His love," I continued. "Sometimes the first experience of God's love comes through another Christian. In fact, Jesus actually once said that the world would know that we are His disciples because of our oneness, our love for one another."[2] Former Nixon aide Charles Colson, in his book *Born Again*, talked about attending his first Washington, D.C., prayer meeting. People were there who had been his political enemies. People were there whom he had harmed because of his previous "tough guy" conduct. Yet love was in that room. There was something that Colson had never before encountered, and that helped change his life.

"God also occasionally 'touches' us with His power as an expression of His love," I told Paul. "Sometimes we feel God's presence as we look at a beautiful sunset or worship Him in song or experience a miracle of physical or emotional healing."

"I don't think I've ever come close to all that," Paul confessed. "Sometimes I wonder whether I've known God at all."

"What do you think is required to know Him?" I asked.

"I'm not sure," he replied. "I've attended church off and on all my life and have always tried to remain conscious of God. I've also tried to be responsive to people's needs. I am involved in several good charities."

"That's all to your credit," I told him, "and shows that you want to do good things. But that does not bridge the gap between man and God."

"What does, then?"

"Jesus does."

"I've heard that before," Paul responded, "but I don't know what it means."

"It means," I replied, "that man is separated from God because of sin and cannot have a relationship with Him unless the sin is dealt with."

"That's great," Paul scowled. "Put me on a guilt trip to try to give me religion."

"If it's true, it's not a guilt trip," I told him. "If it's true, it's the most important admission you will ever make about yourself, and it will prompt you to confess your helplessness to God and to trust Him with His answer to the problem."

I was very candid with Paul and admitted that I'd heard that reaction before. In fact, I said, "I'm fascinated by some people's reluctance to admit that they are sinners and by their resentment of Christians who preach that message. But think about it for a minute. If what God says is true, it provides a lot of understanding about us.

"Let me illustrate.

"What's the most important day in the life of an alcoholic? Isn't it the day that person finally sees the truth and admits that there is a problem? What's the most effective way to help that alcoholic realize the truth? Lovingly tell him. It would be tragic if a doctor avoided telling a patient he has cancer because he didn't want to hurt him. It would be unwise to fail to confront a woman who is physically abusing her children. The pathway to recovery for her would include her realization of what's happening in her life and in her home and her willingness to receive help.

"It's the same in our relationship with God. He has lovingly communicated the truth to us, the truth that sin has spoiled the world and hindered our relationship with Him. Sin had to be dealt with, and Jesus came to deal with it. If we realize that and trust what He did for us, our sin is cleansed and we can come into relationship with

Him. It's no different from having an accurate self-image, a real understanding of what's true."

"I've never seen it that way before," Paul said. "I have to admit that there is plenty of evidence of sin in my life, even though I've resented anybody suggesting that to me." Before our lunch was over, Paul had prayed to God, confessing his realization of being a sinner and of being in need of what the Savior had done for him. He accepted Christ's offer of complete forgiveness.

God has given us the privilege of having relationships with other people who are important in our lives. He has given us a natural hunger for those relationships. He has given us the ability to exchange that kind of love, a rich and warm human love, with each other. But the ultimate hunger is for His love, and we're never quite satisfied until we find it. Perfect unconditional love is God's love. You, too, can stand with uplifted arms and cry, "I am loved by the Almighty God!"

PART FIVE

Balancing Love
and Approval

Chapter Nine

"Which Is Most Important: Love or Approval?"

Sometimes I am asked, "Which is more important, love or approval? If I had to err in one direction or the other, which would be better?"

How would you answer that? Would you say it is better to enter into adulthood knowing you are loved but not knowing how to perform or would it be preferable to be functional without the support of unconditional love?

Most of us would probably say love is the greater priority, and perhaps there is some justification to that. Learning how to perform if you know you are loved is probably easier than learning how to love after you know how to perform. I would argue, however, that neither love nor approval is more important than the other. They are of equal value and any deficiency in one affects the quality of the other.

Let me say at this point that I'm describing ideals. I certainly have not achieved or experienced a perfect balance of love and approval and neither has my wife nor my seven children. Sometimes we don't need to even try to distinguish between them. I don't pause at the moment of expressing something to one of my children and think, *Am I expressing love right now or am I expressing approval? And how can I keep from confusing them?* Most of the time we're probably expressing a mixture of love and approval.

Two of my daughters, Kristi and Karise, love acting and singing and dancing. Recently, they appeared together in a summer stage production. I arranged to attend two of the performances, and no words could describe all that I felt as I sat and watched them. I laughed, I cried, I applauded. I feared that they might forget their lines. I had flashbacks to their childhood; I had visions of their future. It was an intensely emotional experience, and at the end of the final performance, I went backstage and gave them both big hugs and told them how much I loved them and how proud I was of them.

Now, let's be analytical for a moment. Was I expressing love to them? Was I expressing approval? Who cares! I was expressing love *and* approval. It was a loving expression of approval or, maybe, an approving expression of love. I don't really know and I'm not particularly concerned. Problems do not result from occasions of expressing both love and approval. Problems occur when long periods of time go by without the distinctive expression of love, which helps a person feel valued for who he or she is.

LOVE AND APPROVAL AND RESPECT

A balance of love and approval and disapproval is important, because I believe that approval and disapproval actually strengthen love. This can best be summarized by the word *respect*. Love without the balancing effect of approval and disapproval is a love that is not respected. On the other hand, approval and disapproval without love are not respected either.

Remember the story I told about the woman who was having trouble getting her three grown children to take responsibility for their lives? She and her husband had never effectively disciplined their children because they feared that would be unloving. Children who do not receive consistent, fair, and effective discipline from their parents do not respect them or their love.

Husbands and wives who are always smiling and sweet and who never want to upset their spouses frequently get hurt as a result. Why? Their love is not respected.

I recently became reacquainted with an old college friend whom I will call Diane. She asked for an appointment to talk about her marriage. "Butch and I have had trouble, almost from the very beginning," she said. "Over the past couple of years he's been coming home late and has admitted that he's spending time with one of the girls from his office. He claims they haven't gotten involved sexually, but he's unapologetic about their friendship and the fact that they confide in and rely on one another emotionally. He says he needs her."

"What has your response been to all this?" I asked.

"I went to my pastor," Diane replied, "and he said that the only way I was going to win Butch's love was by being submissive and loving to him and trying to attract him back to me." Diane said that she had been doing her best but was getting discouraged because nothing was changing.

"Your husband is doing something destructive to your marriage," I said. "He is accountable to God and to you for how he conducts himself, and I believe you need to respond to this with firmness and with wise disapproval."

"What do you suggest?" she asked.

"Let me ask you a question," I replied, "and give me an honest answer."

"I will."

"If this does not change, what is going to happen to your marriage? What is going to happen in your heart?"

"Frankly, I'm ready to walk out," Diane said. "I know that's not the right thing to do, and my pastor would be disappointed if he knew that was how I felt, but I have to be honest in saying that I'm sick of not having a husband, I'm afraid he has committed adultery, and I can't stand it any-more."

I told Diane that regardless of whether or not her feelings were right, they were her true feel-ings and she needed to realize how important it was to take them seriously. For the previous two years she had buried her feelings and tried to pretend that nothing was wrong.

"What should I do?" she asked.

"Your husband may have some love for you and may sense your love for him," I replied, "but I doubt he has any respect for you or for your love. There hasn't been any strength to it, since he's never had to be accountable to you for his fla-grant violation of your marriage. He can continue living with you and having his flings at the office for as long as he wishes. It isn't expensive for him."

As we continued to talk, Diane realized that she had tolerated the intolerable and had done so out of a sincere desire to do what was right as a Christian. She decided to confront her husband about his behavior and to tell him confidently that she needed him to conduct himself as if he were married to her alone, which he was. If it really was his choice to continue his romantic re-lationship with another person, Diane was going to move in with her father and put some thought and prayer into her future.

At first, Butch didn't take Diane seriously, but after a few days he saw that Diane was not kid-ding and was not going to change her mind. Yet, he kept insisting that he needed both Diane and his girlfriend. Diane kept her word, and one day when Butch came home, she was gone. Butch became furious; however, within a week, he was calling Diane on the phone and trying to talk her into coming back home. "Only if you end your relationship with your girlfriend and are willing to seek counseling with me," Diane insisted.

Within weeks Butch and Diane entered into counseling, he brought his extramarital affair to an end, and he finally went through the severe season of guilt that accompanies the admission of sin and change of conduct. Most importantly, he learned to have respect for his wife's love, which provided a foundation for building the remaining years of their marriage.

The Flip Side

The flip side to this is that approval and disapproval need love in order to be respected and effective. Have you ever noticed that you'll allow your best friend to say truthful and painful things to you, but you won't allow your mother-in-law to make the very same comments? That's because our love qualifies us to disapprove. If you have proven to me that you love me, then you have earned the privilege of criticizing me.

It is of further importance to note that approval and disapproval given without love can, at times, be abusive. I have talked with many parents who have been accused of abusing their children. The factors that produce such a problem are usually rooted in the hurt and the pain of the parents themselves. Those who have never known un-conditional love often can't give such love. Inter-estingly, however, many abusive parents don't realize that the treatment they are dispensing can be classified as abuse. In their minds the parents believe that the children deserve what they are getting and that such disapproval is go-ing to correct their misbehavior. In most cases that's how the parents themselves were treated when they were children. Abuse is a pathological and intense form of a relationship based on ap-proval and disapproval, mostly disapproval, given without love.

In summary, both love and approval (or disap-proval) are vitally important and provide strength to one another. Together they actually promote respect.

WHAT DOES THIS MEAN TO YOU?

All of the conclusions we've reached in this book will be meaningless without one final, rather simple principle that I call "The Impor-tance of Doing."

One afternoon during my radio program, I re-ceived a call which illustrates what I mean.

A grieving father said that his grade-school daughter had been molested by a member of his church. The molester had been arrested and was being prosecuted, but the father commented, "I know I am supposed to forgive him, but I can't."

"Forgiveness is difficult and sometimes requires a long time before it is finished," I replied. "I don't think anyone will fault you in this instance for having a struggle." We talked for several minutes, then I asked, "What have you actually done to forgive this man?"

"I'm not sure what you mean," he replied.

"I can imagine that you've contemplated what you would do to this molester if you ever got your hands on him," I continued, "and most of what you've considered would probably put you in jail."

"You're right there," he said.

"Jesus taught us, however, that we should pray for those who despitefully use us and that we should do good to them, not cause them harm."

"Does that mean the molester should not be in jail?" he asked.

"Not at all," I quickly replied. "It is essential that this man pay for what he has done and get help. That's a matter of justice. But over a period of time, you are going to be the one who is tormented if you do not come to the point of forgiving that man."

"That's the question," the father lamented. "How do I do that?"

"It's not enough to merely feel the conviction that you should forgive," I told him. "You could spend years feeling guilt for your feelings and nothing would change. It's going to be important for you to actually 'do' something in response to your desire to forgive."

"What do you suggest?"

"Have you prayed for the man?"

"No."

"That's the place to begin," I said. "Praying for another person is 'doing'; it is an investment in that person's life, a step beyond simply sitting and feeling guilty for your feelings."

I learned the power of this principle several years ago. A fairly well-known local minister telephoned me and asked if I would write a script for a video presentation for his organization. I was pastoring a small church at the time but because of my experience in media, I often did freelance work to help augment my income. "I'm very busy," I told him, "and don't really have the time, but my family does need some extra support so I'll do it."

I worked hard on the script, writing several drafts and helping to oversee some of the production. The final product was a success. However, the check I had expected for the work never appeared. I waited several weeks but to no avail. I called and wrote. No response. Because of my friendship with the man and because the amount of money owed was not a large sum, I decided against taking any further action. But my resentment remained alive and well. Every time I heard his name or saw his picture, I grumbled inside. Whenever things got tight financially, I would think about how nice it would be to have that money.

One afternoon I was sitting in my office and felt myself beginning to steam about the situation again when I remembered how important it had been in the past for me to "do" something in response to what I felt was right. I had the impression that I ought to send a donation to the preacher's organization. "No," I told myself. "He owes me money! I don't owe him anything. I'm not going to send any donation to him!"

Then I realized how much torment I had been through because of my resentment. I reflected on the fact that obeying Jesus' command would probably release me from that torment. I pulled out my checkbook, wrote a check for fifteen dollars, put it into an envelope, and then walked to a nearby mailbox to mail it. At that moment of "doing," my bitterness was released. As I walked back to my office, I felt a softening and even a taste of victory. For the previous weeks, I had felt that my friend "had" me. Now, I "had" him. What could not be accomplished by days and nights of guilt and good intentions had been resolved by an actual act of "doing." My opinion of him had not changed. I still felt he had done wrong. But my attitude had been changed, and I was no longer imprisoned.

Perhaps you have felt a stirring in your heart as we have discussed love, approval, and disapproval. You've hungered to love and be loved. You've decided that disapproval is a valuable thing. You've prayed for a relationship with God.

Don't let what you feel inside remain trapped there. Don't get caught in the trap of "intentions." It is important that you take whatever you've been inspired to do and actually *do* it. Instead of privately grieving over a lack of love in your life, step out and practice *doing* acts of love, acts of acknowledging a person because of who that person is. Instead of saying, "Yes, someday I need to approve of those around me," go ahead and *do* it.

Doing takes determination and commitment— the determination to apply these principles to each of the hundreds of times a week we relate to our husbands and wives, our children, our co-workers, and our friends and the commitment to always think, *Am I treating my (husband, wife, child, co-worker, friend) as I'd like to be treated?* It won't be any easier for you than it was for me to apply these principles to my minister friend's owing me money. But if you really believe them, if you really feel that God wishes you to live this way, it's worth the effort. Every day on my radio show, "Talk from the Heart," I renew my commitment to expressing love and approval as I talk to people whose lives have been damaged by a lack of love. You might renew your commitment every so often by rereading portions of this book.

Jesus once gave to His followers a message, which contained a lot of important teachings. At the end of the message, He told a story about a man who built his house on a foundation of sand. When the storms came and the winds blew, the house was demolished. A second man, however, built his house on a foundation of rock and it survived the storms. Jesus said the second man was an example of people who heard His teachings and *did* them. He advocated the importance of "doing."[1]

Love and approval and disapproval are vitally important concepts, which powerfully affect our feelings about ourselves and others. I pray that you will be able to experience love and approval rather than simply be inspired by them. I pray you will be able to love and feel loved—with no strings attached.

Notes

Chapter 2

1. Matthew 21:31.

Chapter 5

1. Proverbs 9:8, 9.
2. Matthew 7:12.

Chapter 6

1. Matthew 18:15-17.

Chapter 8

1. 1 John 4:10 (NIV).
2. John 17:21.

Chapter 9

1. Matthew 7:24-27.

About the Author

RICH BUHLER hosts the nationally syndicated, daily radio talk program, "Talk From the Heart," which originates from KBRT-AM in Los Angeles. He is also the host of two award-winning films, *Fractured Families* and *They Lied to Us*.

Rich's varied background includes nearly twenty years of ministry and professional broadcast experience. He has worked as a writer, editor, producer, and on-air personality in Los Angeles, including positions with Westinghouse Broadcasting (KFWB) and CBS (KNX).

A graduate of Biola University in California, Rich has served in several pastoral positions in churches, including more than six years as senior pastor in Long Beach, California. Rich and his wife, Linda, who is a musician and popular women's speaker, live with their seven children in Westminister, California. Rich's hobbies include flying (he is an active pilot), fishing, cooking, reading, and traveling.